A Year in a
LAKE DISTRICT GARDEN

Sue Tasker

Published by Sigma Leisure – an imprint of
Sigma Press, 1 South Oak Lane, Wilmslow, Cheshire SK9 6AR, England.

British Library Cataloguing in Publication Data
A CIP record for this book is available from the British Library.

ISBN: 1-85058-762-0

Typesetting and Design by: Sigma Press, Wilmslow, Cheshire.

Cover Design: Belvoir Cartographics & Design

Illustrations: Christine Isherwood

Photographs: the author, except where indicated

Cover photographs: clockwise from top left: 1. *Geranium* 'Russell Prichard' and the lodge at Brockhole 2. Entrance to the kitchen garden *(Graham Beech)* 3. *Crinodendron hookerianum* and *Iris sibirica* 'White Swirl' 4. A view of Brockhole house from the meadow

Printed by: MFP Design & Print

Preface

Gardeners' lives are regulated by the seasons of the year and ruled by the weather. This book is a record of one gardener's year, in a corner of the country renowned for the natural beauty of its landscape, for the lushness of its gardens, and for its huge amounts of rainfall!

The main text is selected from a series of weekly articles, written for the *Westmorland Gazette* between 1998 and 2000. The articles cover a wide range of subjects, and give an insight into the day to day running of both the gardens at Brockhole and my own garden in Cockermouth. Each chapter covers a month of the year, with a comprehensive list of 'Jobs for the gardener' at the end of each month.

The information and anecdotes in this book are based on over 25 years of gardening experience, fourteen of them spent working in Cumbria. The photographs were mostly taken at Brockhole and help to illustrate the variety and wealth of plants that can be grown in this mild, moist part of the world.

The gardens at Brockhole were laid out around one hundred years ago by the landscape architect, Thomas Mawson, for the Gaddum family who made their home here in 1899. Together they built a series of south and west facing terraces which slope gently down to the shores of Windermere, and which move from formal to informal planting, through flower beds, meadow and woodland to the lakeshore.

During the fifteen years to 2001, the gardens have been carefully restored, with many of Mawson's original ideas and garden furnishings being re-introduced. The plantings, whilst still in keeping with Mawson's ideals, have continued to evolve, and Brockhole is now home to numerous interesting and unusual plants from all over the world. The sheltered nature of the garden, the acidic soil and the mild, moist climate of South Lakeland means that a number of slightly tender plants have also found a place here.

Mawson's original plantings that still remain include some fine specimen trees, both conifers and broadleaves, formal clipped yew and box hedging, rhododendrons, wisteria and magnolias. To these have been added a wealth of herbaceous plantings, scented plants, old-fashioned roses and various other ornamental trees and shrubs designed to provide something of interest at all times of the year.

Brockhole grounds cover an area of around thirty acres, with ten acres of formal gardens, ten of meadow and ten of woodland. They are open to the public all year round.

Sue Tasker
Brockhole

Contents

* * *

Autobiography

* * *

January

The start of a new year and I am filled with ideas and enthusiasm for the seasons to come. It never seems to matter if last year was too wet or too dry, or if things didn't grow well or were ravaged by pests; by January there is the chance for a completely fresh start, the promise of the perfect garden. Slowly, the days begin to lengthen, and the sun (when we see it) has a little warmth to it. There is always the possibility of snow, though most years it is confined to the high fells, where it adds another dimension to the views over the lake from the garden terraces.

Spring bulbs

What a relief after so much winter weather, to see the first bulbs beginning to flower: snowdrops, aconites, and on my windowsill at home the first rich blue *Iris reticulata*, boldly showing off despite the wind and rain. These smart little irises, no more than four to six inches tall, are quite hardy and can be grown in the open ground. Whenever I have tried this however, mine have flowered once and then disappeared, whether due to slugs, or mice, or rot from too much damp I am not quite sure. I have found that they last much longer if planted in tubs or window boxes – when they have finished flowering they can be left in situ to die down for the summer. At the same time, the containers can be used for summer bedding, if care is taken not to damage the iris bulbs when planting.

Speaking of bulbs, the latest bulb catalogues have arrived. They are full of mouth-watering goodies which, if planted in the next few weeks will flower in the summer and autumn. Gladioli are very much in evidence, as are begonias and dahlias, but the section that most interests me is the one marked Miscellaneous Bulbs. Here are to be found such horticultural gems as the Peruvian daffodil, tiger flowers and Californian hyacinths. I shall be investing in some nerines, bulbs that produce tall

umbels of soft pink flowers in October and November. They are not quite hardy, so I shall plant them in pots that can be overwintered in the shed or cold greenhouse. As they come into flower they can be used to decorate the terrace or dropped into any empty spaces in the autumn border.

A subject that is also in my thoughts at the moment, though for quite different reasons, is the disposal of woody waste in the garden. The clippings and prunings from trees and shrubs can easily accumulate into quite a stack by the end of the winter and it is sometimes difficult to know what to do with them all. In the past, the answer was easy – you simply had a bonfire and burnt the lot. This practice is becoming environmentally frowned upon, and we must begin to look for alternatives. One simple option is to create a 'habitat pile'. This entails nothing more taxing than cutting the material into suitable lengths and stacking it closely together in an out of the way place. If you are lucky, it will be used for shelter by hedgehogs and other passing animals, and as a safe nesting place for small birds. It will slowly rot away, providing a home for insects and fungi that will in turn attract more wildlife to your garden.

The second alternative is to shred or chip the woody waste. This will reduce your huge mound of unwanted prunings to a small pile of useful chippings in a short but noisy space of time. The chippings can be used directly on the ground as an informal footpath surface, or they can be rotted down and used as garden mulch or compost. Shredders and chippers come in a wide range of sizes and prices, but if you don't want to buy one they are available for hire at most tool-hire shops. Perhaps you could share the cost with a friend or neighbour. Not quite the same as standing round the bonfire together but never mind ...

Helleborus foetidus

'Stinking hellebore' is hardly the most prepossessing of common names; indeed in comparison to the common names of its close relatives, the Christmas rose and the Lenten rose, it is positively insulting! It is not even particularly descriptive like the names of its other cousins, the Corsican hellebore and the green hellebore,

Helleborus foetidus 'Westerflisk'

for the flowers of *Helleborus foetidus* do not smell nasty, rather they are usually pleasant smelling.

Flowering as it does in the middle of winter, *Helleborus foetidus* has a special place in my heart. From early December through to May, it produces generous clusters of pale green,

 *3*

bell-shaped flowers, each with a delicate purple margin to the edge of the bell. Behind each group of flowers are clusters of large, light green bracts, giving the flower spike an even fuller appearance. The leaves of the stinking hellebore are dark green, about 9 inches long, each with 7 to 10 lobes like a many-fingered hand. It is these leaves that give rise to the common name, they give off a rather unpleasant smell if crushed. The whole plant is generally between 2 and 3 feet tall with a spread of about 18 inches. It is technically a 'perennial herb', but this is confusing as the leaves and stems are present throughout the winter months, being shed and replaced in late summer after the seeds have set.

Helleborus foetidus is a European native, growing as far south as Portugal and as far north as Northern Germany, as low as at sea level and as high up as 2100 metres. I have seen it growing wild in hedgerows and scrubby woodland in Gloucestershire, where it is a wonderful sight in flower. The wild plants are usually found on chalky or limestone soils, though I have grown it fairly successfully in acid soil at Brockhole for some ten years or so. The handsome variety *H. foetidus* 'Westerflisk', which has reddish stems and leaves with a purplish tinge, may be more particular; despite cosseting it only lasted a couple of years before giving up the ghost! Hellebores in general are tough plants that will tolerate a wide variety of conditions. They do appreciate a soil rich in humus and organic matter, and like many plants, prefer to be neither too dry nor completely waterlogged. The only pests I have found on them have been aphids and tiny snails, neither of which was anything to worry about.

It's an ill wind ...

With so much wet weather and so many high winds, it is difficult to find a good reason to go out into the garden, never mind to be enthusiastic enough to write encouraging things about it! It's an ill wind that blows no good though; Boxing Day gales blew over a medium-sized conifer that was growing in a side border at Brockhole. I had never really liked it, but had equally never had quite enough reason to chop it down; now that nature has done the dirty work for me I can revel in the extra light and space created without any of the accompanying guilt!

I wonder how many of us live with inconveniently placed, or over-mature shrubs and trees, because we are too sentimental to cut them down and start again. Sometimes we are so used to seeing a particular plant in a particular place that we can't imagine what it would be like without it, even when the results of its removal would be a huge improvement. It might pay to get into the habit of trying to justify the position of each plant every few years or so; is it still worthy of a place in the garden or is it just taking up space? Would it look better somewhere else, and would something else look better in its place? If I had applied this test to my fallen evergreen, it might not have lasted quite so long!

By coincidence, growing beside this wind-blown conifer are some of the few plants that are worth venturing out in the cold to see at this time of the year. As I raked up the wreckage left after clearing away the biggest branches, I also raked away the fallen leaves that were covering our largest group of aconites. And there they were, looking bright, buttery yellow and so spring-like that for a while I felt that winter must soon be over! Aconites grow each year from tubers, and it is possible to buy and plant dormant tubers from bulb companies. I have never had much success with these; by far the most effective way of starting a new clump, or increasing an existing group, is to divide existing plants immediately after flowering, before the leaves start to fade.

Not far from the aconites are several species of willow, grown for their catkins, with buds just beginning to think about opening. *Salix aegyptica* is often the first to show its large grey and yellow catkins, but it can be beaten by *Salix koriyanagi*. The slender catkins of this willow are an attractive pink and grey against the fresh green of its stems. But my affections are reserved for another Japanese willow that is just coming into flower, *Salix* 'Melanostachys'. These catkins are glossy black at first, becoming suffused with bright red as the anthers appear. Finally the whole catkin turns yellow as the pollen is produced; a brilliant display! If you see a willow flowering that you like, it is

worth begging a cutting from the owner; willows are amongst the easiest of cuttings to root. Put them in a pot of compost and grit in the cold frame or just dibble them in, in an out of the way spot in the garden. They will take a few months to root and then they can be transplanted to their proper place in the autumn. Willows will even root in a jug of water; the first cuttings I ever made (at about the age of 10), were some goat willow stems from a local hedgerow, rooted in a jar on the windowsill at home.

Blackberries or Brambles?

Blackberries and brambles are two different common names for the same plant, *Rubus fruticosus*. Whilst the first name conjures up images of fruit pies and Sunday afternoons spent wandering along the hedgerows of a country lane looking for these tasty fruits, the second name implies something altogether more sinister!

Brambles can grow at up to two inches a day, and their sole aim appears to be to cover as much ground, in as short a time, as possible. To the gardener, especially those with shrub beds or any kind of rough grass, hedges or woodland, this can only mean trouble. Armed with sharp, backward pointing spines, and rooting into the ground at intervals along the extending stems, brambles that are left to take hold can soon produce an impenetrable and unsightly tangle of smothering growth, rapidly taking over neglected areas and scrambling energetically through shrub borders and wooded areas. The winter months are a good time to hunt them out, when their semi-evergreen foliage is more obvious against bare shrubs. In the past, because of constraints of time and manpower, I have tried to control patches of brambles by cutting them down to ground level. This is fine as long as they are cut several times each year, in which case they will gradually disappear. But cut them only once a year and they will spring back again with renewed vigour, and worse – they will scramble over the dead, cut stems from the previous cutting and make an even thicker thicket than before.

There are several chemicals on the market that can be used to control brambles, they are quite strong and must be used exactly according to the manufacturer's instructions. They may need more than one application to eradicate the problem. Not being a big fan of chemicals, my preferred method of control is to dig the beggars out! Ideally this should be done whenever you notice an invading plant; leave it for a couple of weeks and the problem will be 28 inches larger all round! Realistically the winter months are the best time to dig out brambles. It is cold enough to don the thorn-proof clothing and thick gloves needed, and the ground is soft and wet enough to enable the roots to pull out more easily. It is important to use a sharp spade, and to make sure you get the roots and crown of the plant out completely. Brambles like nothing better than to snap off at ground level, leaving the crown of the plant ready for another attack as soon as your back is turned. Dig or pull them up, making sure the roots come out cleanly, following each stem to the end to find and remove any rooted runners. Tackled in the right frame of mind, this can be a really satisfying winter job, extracting stems of up to 20 feet in length and rapidly uncovering large tracts of lost land. (I say 'in the right frame of mind', because tackled on a bad day this spiky task can be the last straw!)

Not all brambles are such a pain however. There are several species that are grown on purpose in gardens, whose flowers or stems are ornamental and whose habits are not quite so invasive as their native cousin, the blackberry. They all belong to the genus *Rubus*, but they came from as far apart as China, the Himalayas, Taiwan and North America.

The flowers of *Rubus* 'Benenden' are as large and as elegant as single white roses, produced each spring and early summer. The plant is a robust, arching shrub that needs plenty of space to grow to its full ten feet of height and spread. Smaller, with more delicate, rose-pink flowers, is the flowering raspberry *Rubus odoratus*. This flowers from early summer until autumn, producing inedible red fruits after flowering. If it's winter colour you are wanting then look no further than *Rubus biflorus*, *R. cockburnianus* and *R. thibetanus*. All these three have erect, prickly stems covered in a brilliant, dusty-white bloom. They look great against a dark background of conifers or evergreen shrubs and can be used (mindful of their prickles!) in winter flower arrangements. To keep them strong and fresh, they should be cut down each year after flowering, encouraging them to grow strong new shoots in time for the winter months.

Rubus tricolor is a low-growing ground cover bramble with dark green, heart-shaped leaves on stems that are covered with rich red bristles. Whilst the previously mentioned plants prefer a sunny position, *R. tricolor* will grow well in shade, quickly forming a low, impenetrable barrier to weeds and unwanted plants. Its chief attraction is the young shoots, which are covered in bright red bristles. To keep a steady supply of these young shoots it is advisable to cut the plant down to ground level every couple of years or so.

Yews

On a flying visit to the gardens at Bodnant in North Wales, I was struck by the size and magnificence of several yew trees growing close to the house. In contrast to the surrounding borders, which were looking dull and wintry, the yews were covered in a brilliant display of bright red berries. Yew trees are dioecious, that is there are separate male and female plants. The males produce small yellow cones bearing pollen in spring, whilst the insignificant female flowers develop into scarlet fruits or arils each autumn. So these were females, 30 to 40 feet tall and a sight to stop visitors in their tracks.

Yews can live for hundreds of years, as can be seen by those growing in the gardens of Levens Hall. They are often seen in formal gardens as topiary specimens, taking easily to clipping and shaping, and having the ability to regrow from old wood after very hard pruning. It is commonly thought that, because they live to such great ages, yews are very slow growing; this is not true of young plants, which may grow between 6 and 12 inches per year and can produce a respectable hedge in under 10 years. The English yew, *Taxus baccata*, is, as its common name suggests, a British native, occurring naturally throughout Europe and North Africa. Many of its cultivars are female forms, though they will only produce arils if there is a nearby male to

Monkey puzzle tree and yew balls at Brockhole

pollinate them. The most common cultivar is *T. baccata* 'Fastigiata' or Irish yew; it is an upright form that grows naturally to a small and graceful columnar tree. The yew topiary balls on the main terrace at Brockhole are made of Irish yew; planted by the Gaddum family at the turn of the last century they have been regularly clipped and are still less than 10 feet tall.

There are golden forms of the common yew; *Taxus baccata* 'Dovastonii Aurea' is a terrible mouthful for this elegant small tree, its new shoots are golden yellow whilst the older, greener leaves are edged with yellow. *T. baccata* 'Fastigiata Aurea' is a yellow form of the Irish yew whilst *T.b.* 'Fastigiata Aureomarginata' has green leaves with golden margins. *Cephalotaxus*, the plum yew, is a distant cousin of the English yew, and can be used to outwit visiting gardening enthusiasts. Its foliage and habit are just like those of normal yew, except that the leaflets are several times larger than those of the latter. It is reputed to make a good hedging plant, though I have only ever seen individual specimens.

Decorative bark and stems

Whilst visiting my parents-in-law each Christmas, my eye is drawn to an unusual shrub in their Gloucestershire garden. It is the contorted hazel Corylus avellana 'Contorta' whose twisted and bent twigs make it look oddly sick and distorted during the summer months. For this reason, I have never had much inclination to plant one, but looking at it without its leaves I could be persuaded otherwise. The twigs, seen clearly without the leaves, are a rich brown colour, twisted into all sorts of wonderful shapes, each one hung with pale yellow catkins. It is a shrub much loved by flower arrangers, which is why my mother-in-law grows it, and as a plant for providing winter colour in the garden it is one of the best.

There are several other trees and shrubs whose best side is seen when the leaves have fallen and there are fewer bright and gaudy summer flowers around to distract our attention. Two of my favourites are small maples, *Acer davidii* and *Acer griseum*. The common name for the first is the snakebark maple, its trunk and branches are striped bright green and white like the skin of a snake. The second maple is the paper-bark, its trunk and branches are a rich orange-brown, the bark peeling and flaking to reveal fresh bright colours beneath. Ornamental cherries are amongst the ranks of trees with decorative bark, the most commonly planted being *Prunus serrula*, whose red-brown bark can look as if it has been polished with furniture wax! At Brockhole we have planted a specimen of *Prunus maackii* which has bark of a rich apricot-brown, I think it will flake and peel as the tree matures.

For those with smaller gardens, there are several shrubs with coloured bark and stems. The dogwoods comprise a large group, the most colourful of which is *Cornus alba* together with its cultivated varieties. The winter stems of *Cornus alba* are bright red, *C.a.* 'Elegantissima' is even richer in colour. *C.a.* 'Kesselringii' has deep purple stems, whilst the stems of *C.a.* 'Sibirica' are a paler scarlet. In contrast, the stems of *Cornus stolonifera* 'Flaviramea' are a bright, greenish yellow; the two species look great growing next to each other. It's only the newest stems that have these really bright colours, they are faded in older branches. The trick to keeping a steady supply of young growth is to cut the plants right down to within a few inches of the ground, each spring just as the leaves are coming out. The plants will then put their energies into producing a whole bunch of new stems, which will be 3-4 feet tall by the end of the season, and as bright a winter colour as you could wish for.

Not to be outdone, the willows also have a candidate for the winter stem market. It is *Salix alba* var. *vitellina* the golden willow, and its vigorous young stems are bright orange-yellow in winter. It also needs to be cut back hard in spring to encourage the new shoots (which may grow to over 6 feet tall in as many months), though it is traditional to leave a short "trunk" of 2-3 feet, which the stems are stooled back to, rather than cutting back to ground level.

Some time during January each year I like to cut a big bunch of these winter stems for the house, mixed with some witch hazel and the colourful berries of *Iris foetidissima*. It serves as a reminder that winter will not last forever and that spring, with its new growth and fresh colours, is only just around the corner!

Jobs for January

❀ Remember to put out food and water for the birds; this can be a difficult time of year for them and a garden full of birds is almost as good as a garden full of flowers.

❀ Keep warm and improve your garden compost by turning over the compost heap

❀ Try not to walk on wet or waterlogged soil and lawns. If you must cross them, put down boards to spread your weight and protect the soil structure.

❀ Watch out for groups of snails overwintering under stones and in cracks in the garden walls. Crush them now! It will make life easier in the spring.

❀ Rake leaves carefully away from clumps of snowdrops, replanting any that have been lifted by frost.

❀ Freshen beds and borders planted with spring flowers by lightly forking over the surface. This not only looks good, showing off the plants to their best advantage, it also helps excess water to drain away.

❀ Check the ties on wall plants and climbers, replace any that have come loose in gales.

❀ Give tools a thorough cleaning, oiling metal surfaces to discourage rusting. Oil the moving parts of secateurs and loppers, sharpen blades and give the tool store a good tidying.

❀ Look closely at fences, pergolas, trellises and other wooden structures. Damage caused by high winds or heavy falls of snow should be put right as soon as possible.

❀ Plant out bowls of daffodils and hyacinths when they have finished flowering in the house, before they have a chance to dry out. Planted in an out of the way spot, they may flower again next year.

February

Winter projects are well under way, and we can begin to see the results of a hard winter's work. Fencing, path construction, paving, rejuvenating beds and borders, tree and shrub planting and pruning, and trellis building are all jobs that keep us busy during the late winter, along with seed sowing and the usual tidying and cutting down of flower and shrub beds.

This is a lean time for garden birds, so we take care to keep feeders regularly topped up. In the borders things are beginning to stir, and for the plant-starved gardener there is light at the end of winter's long tunnel.

The woodland garden

A few years ago we converted one of the rhododendron beds at Brockhole into a woodland border. For some time we had been looking for space to grow more woodland plants, the species that require light shade and a moist, humus-rich soil, prevented from becoming waterlogged by the root systems of surrounding trees and shrubs. We chose this particular bed because some of the rhododendrons growing in it had passed their prime, and one or two were suffering from a variety of mildew that spoils the leaves and reduces flowering. These sickly plants were removed and the bottom branches of the remaining shrubs were pruned away to reveal their trunks. Many species of rhododendron have quite decorative bark that is generally hidden under the lower branches, so this in itself was a new addition to the bed.

The result of all this thinning and pruning was a much more open border, with room to plant an understorey of shade lovers, protected from too much sunlight by a canopy of rhododendron, *Crinodendron* and *Cotinus* foliage. The first plants to go in were snowdrops and aconites, together with some clumps of spring-flowering *Pulmonaria*. I hope that these will eventually spread to form larger drifts, providing masses of early colour. Next we planted some *Meconopsis grandis*, the blue poppies that

are a talking point in early summer. They are short-lived perennials and may have to be replaced every few years, but this is a small price to pay for such wonderful flowers! Another unusual plant, *Hacquetia epipactis*, given to me by some friends a few years previously and struggling to survive in its original planting place, surprised me by growing away rapidly when moved to the woodland border. It now covers an area of several square feet, its little yellow flowers surrounded by collars of bright green bracts are just coming into bloom. Which only goes to show that it is worth trying ailing plants in several different positions to see if one will suit them better than another.

The shady soil, rich in leaf mould and humus, makes a natural seedbed, and some plants have arrived in the border uninvited. Tidying through it this week I have had to weed out seedlings of ivy, holly and berberis. Lots of foxgloves have turned up too, and as I am quite fond of them I have left them in places where there is room, only weeding out those in inconvenient places. *Disporum smithii*, a tough little plant with creamy, trumpet-shaped flowers followed by bright orange berries, has also dropped its seeds into the bed. These are just beginning to germinate, looking like so many bean sprouts lying in the soil.

There is quite a way to go yet before we fill this new bed, but the process continues to be an interesting and rewarding one – far more exciting than a bed full of rhododendrons.

More hellebores

The Christmas roses, *Helleborus niger*, began flowering in the garden at Brockhole during early December. On my wanderings round the garden this week (the first week of February) I notice that they are still flowering, and still looking good despite some munching from a slug or two and some mud splashing from the rain.

Now however, they are joined by a couple of other species of hellebore that are just beginning to flower, and that I hope will last as long as their winter cousins. The first that I noticed was the Lenten lily, *Helleborus orientalis*. We have several plants of this species, given to me many years ago by Chris Crowder from

Levens Hall. They were grown from seed rather than from divisions and as such show a wide range of what is known as "seedling variation". The most obvious difference is that some are maroon and some are creamy white, but look more closely and there are many differences in the size, shape and colour of the internal markings as well. On close inspection the insides of these Lenten lilies are really pretty, they can be more fully appreciated by cutting a few flower heads and floating them in a bowl of water, where they will last for several days

As an added bonus, if they are happy in your garden, Lenten lilies will seed themselves around and produce even more variations on the basic theme. I am hoping ours will eventually form a carpet, and I have planted some bulbs of the spring snowflake, *Leucojum aestivum*, in amongst the young seedlings that are shooting up. The plan is that the white, cream, maroon and pink of the hellebores will look even more dazzling with these huge green and white snowdrops growing beside them.

The second species of hellebore flowering now is the charmingly named stinking hellebore, *Helleborus foetidus*. The deeply divided, dark green leaves of this plant are the perfect background for showing off the cup-shaped, pale green flowers. They hang in small clusters, each flower edged delicately with a thin red margin. I have never been able to detect any bad smell from this plant, though I did once get a nasty nettle rash on my fingertips from collecting and opening seedpods. It is perhaps worth mentioning here that I later discovered parts of some hellebores, particularly the roots, can be poisonous if eaten, and they should not be grown where cattle might graze on them.

Many garden plants have some poisonous properties, especially if eaten, and there has been an increased awareness of this in the nursery and garden centre trade in recent years. It is now quite common to see plants for sale labelled as irritant or poisonous. My own view is that by labelling those we know to be dangerous we are implying that those that are not labelled are safe to eat. In fact, this is far from the case, as many plants have never been tested, and could be just as dangerous as those that are labelled. Far better to instil caution into our children (and

animals) by not allowing them to put any plants into their mouths unless they are tried and tested fruit or vegetables!

Witch hazel

As a child I can remember having witch hazel liquid dabbed onto bruises and sprains; it had an odd, astringent smell and a pleasant, cooling effect on the offending injury. Nowadays when I think of witch hazel, I more often think of the plants from which this liquid is obtained, and the rich scent of the flowers that brightens otherwise dull winter days. Witch hazel is the common name for a group of shrubs more correctly known as *Hamamelis*, that are so unlike any other shrubs they have their own plant family, the Hamamelidaceae. They come China and Japan, and also from North America, and have been grown in this country since the early 1700s. The first to arrive was *H. virginiana*, discovered by early settlers to North America, who used its branches for water divining rods and learned to distil the medicinal oil from its leaves and bark.

The most beautiful of the witch hazels, *Hamamelis mollis*, was introduced to this country from China by Augustine Henry in 1888. It has rich, golden yellow flowers with narrow, strap-shaped petals, not unlike brightly coloured spiders. Because they are produced from December to February, the flowers stand out against the bare branches, and if by chance you should fail to notice them, they are armed with a delicious scent designed to halt you in your tracks. As an added bonus, the broad oval leaves provide excellent autumn colour, in shades of orange, yellow and red. The Japanese witch hazel, *H. japonica*, is similar to the Chinese version, whilst the hybrid between the two, *H. x intermedia*, has produced some marvellous red and coppery orange cultivars such as 'Jelena', 'Vezna' and 'Diane'.

All these plants are perfectly hardy in this country, and look well either as specimen shrubs or as part of a shrub border. Relatively slow growing at first, (especially if grazed by deer as some of mine have been!) they may eventually reach a height and spread of 12 to 15 feet, but they can easily be pruned after flowering to keep them smaller. *Hamamelis* like a moderately

Hamamelis mollis

rich soil, moist but not too wet, with an acid or neutral pH. They will do well in full sun or partial shade, but they will not like a site exposed to cold winds.

Garden edges

At this time of year, when the autumn leaves are under control, most of the borders have been cut down and tidied up, and our winter projects are well under way, I like to spend some time looking at the edges of the garden. Firstly, there are the edges of the lawns and borders. As the year goes on these edges become squashed down by the mowers and thus more difficult to clip.

Now, when the soil is soft and moist, is one of the best times to straighten and crisp up these edges, using a sharp spade or a half-moon cutter. When straightening wobbly edges, use a plank or line for a straightedge, for curved edges use a thick piece of rope or hosepipe as a guide. When you come to clip these new edges next spring they will be a pleasure to cut rather than a chore.

Secondly, there are the edges of the garden in general. I suspect most of us have areas of the garden that we don't get to very often, where things are generally left to look after themselves. This is fine, and these areas are often valuable havens for wildlife, but they do need the occasional overhaul to prevent them from getting completely out of control. Cut back any large or overhanging shrubs, check that boundary fences are sound, keep access pathways clear and then forget about them for another year!

Then there are the "edges" of your gardening activities, the chores that there will be little time for once the growing season starts. I like to check over all our tools at this time of year, mending broken ones, ordering new where repairs are impractical. Buying in a good supply of potting compost before the seeds arrive is a useful move, nothing is more irritating than running out of compost in the middle of sowing or potting. Check supplies of pots, string, canes, fertiliser and anything else used on a regular basis. The mowing season is sneaking up on us gradually, so this is a good time to wheel the mower out of the shed and see if it will start or not. If you gave it a good clean and service before putting it away, it should be fine; otherwise now is the time to change the oil and fit a new spark plug if it is petrol-powered, or to check the condition of cables, plugs, fuses and circuit breaker if it is an electrical model. Those who still have a push mower will have no such problems, but all models will need to have the condition of the blades checked; oiling, sharpening or replacing blunt or broken blades now will save time and frustration later.

Hedge planting

As part of a project to upgrade our car park at Brockhole for visitors with disabilities, the gardeners have planted a mixed hedge, something like 300 feet long. It is made up of native species, including holly, hawthorn, blackthorn, hazel, yew and wild roses. At intervals along the hedge we have planted some damson trees, raised for the Westmorland Damson Association as part of a remarkable regeneration project.

Damsons have traditionally been grown in the Lyth and Winster Valleys for over 300 years, with many thousands of trees producing a crop that was made into wine, beer, gin, jam, ice cream, damson cheese and other delicacies. The trees themselves were, and still are to some extent, a tourist attraction in their own right, being a marvellous sight when in flower. Over the last 50 years the number of trees has declined dramatically, and the Westmorland Damson Association was formed to resurrect the industry and market its products in order to boost the local economy.

The first hurdle was to find a supply of tree seedlings. Damson stones are very difficult to germinate, and although cuttings will eventually root, they are tricky and it can be hard to find enough material to take them in bulk. So members of the Association collected over 1000 stones and sent them to a specialist firm for germinating. The stones were then sent to another firm to be grown on into small trees about 14 inches tall, when they were returned to the Association for distributing.

On a completely different note, my 'plant of the moment' is *Garrya elliptica*, the silk tassel bush. A native of western USA, this evergreen shrub was introduced to Britain in 1828. It is grown primarily for the catkins produced by the male plants (those of the female are generally less showy and hence they are seldom grown.) These catkins are between 6 and 8 inches long, grey-green in colour and generously covered with yellow anthers each winter. The main snag with *Garrya* is that it is not reliably hardy, it needs to be planted snugly amongst other shrubs or against a wall for extra protection from cold weather. The sight of its flamboyant catkins, produced so bravely in the middle of each winter, is enough to convince me that it is worth the risk.

Slides and photographs

Over the winter months I like to spend some time sorting and filing my modest collection of slides. For years, I have kept the slides in their original boxes, having to sort laboriously through them each time I needed a particular picture. Now they are all in plastic envelopes, in sheets of 20, and can be easily viewed by putting whole sheets against a light source. The most interesting thing about this exercise is the way it has allowed me to compare photographs of the same view or plant, taken several years apart. How easy it is to forget what a particular bed or area used to look like, how quickly (or slowly) a tree or shrub grows, and how all things, including the gardeners, change over the years!

There are slides from my first couple of years at Brockhole, clearing out the kitchen garden, putting up trellises, erecting the wooden pergola and planting new plants throughout the garden. Then there are slides of these areas as they began to blend in, and the new plants began to fill their allotted spaces. Then there are slides of us thinning the same borders, hard-pruning shrubs and replanting once more! There are pictures of hostas, their leaves unspoilt by slugs and snails, in the days before we gave up using slug pellets and tried to become more environmentally friendly. There are photos of trees that have succumbed to winter gales and are now no more than rotting stumps. There are pictures of pathetically small trees, newly planted, that are now respectably into double figures in both years and in feet. And there are views of the house and gardens that must have looked much the same for the last hundred years, since Thomas Mawson first laid out the gardens and the Gaddum family lived here.

There are many pictures missing – those I forgot to take; of particular days or events, particular plants, people who worked with us and people who visited. I wish I had made more of an effort with 'before' and 'after' shots of work in progress, and I wish I were a better photographer so that the shots I did take were clearer, brighter or more atmospheric. But the fact remains that this is a personal record of the garden (and my working life) since 1987; it is a fascinating, if slightly motley, collection of pictures that I am glad I have taken the trouble to sort through. I will be taking more trouble in the future to add to this collection, and to keep up with my cataloguing.

Protective clothing

What do you wear on your feet whilst gardening? For years, I wore wellington boots and, of course, no matter how many layers of socks I wore in winter my feet were always cold! Then I moved on to leather boots, which were heavier and less water-proof but definitely warmer. Better still, I now discover, are the new breeds of walking boots, that weigh very little and have complete waterproofing – Goretex, Sympatex and so on. Quite expensive I agree, but getting cheaper, and a by-product of the waterproofing is that they are very warm in cold weather! If you are using any kind of machinery, such as a lawn mower, then it is good sense to protect your feet with the stoutest boots you have, even in hot weather. And, if you are moving anything heavy such as paving slabs, then boots with steel toe-caps are a must. I used to laugh at the stories of people sticking forks into their feet whilst digging, but it is quite possible, I *have* done it myself, and strong footwear will protect your pride as well as your feet.

Whilst we are on the subject of protective clothing, I am often shocked by the number of people (some of them "Professionals") who use chain saws without adequate protection. The recom-mended gear is based on a material called Kevlar, which will tangle in the blade of the saw and stop it running if the material is cut into. A chain saw operator should wear Kevlar-padded trousers, stout gloves with Kevlar backs, a helmet with ear-defenders and mesh visor, and boots with steel toe-caps and Kevlar padding. All this sounds cumbersome and expensive, but a chain saw is a potentially lethal weapon that cannot be expected to know the difference between the branch of a tree and your arm or leg! It is also very noisy and sends out plenty of chips and sawdust, so it makes sense to protect eyes and ears too. If you hire a saw, you should be able to hire the protective gear that goes with it for a small extra fee; it could save your life!

Chemicals are a less obvious, but more sinister danger; they can seep through your skin, accumulating in the body and

causing health problems years later. So again it makes sense to use protective clothing; farming and agricultural merchants sell inexpensive, chemical-proof gloves, boots and overalls, with goggles or visors to protect the eyes from splashes. If you get into the habit of wearing them every time you use chemicals, then it's not much more of a chore than remembering to put on those warm boots on a chilly morning.

Corylus maxima 'Purpurea'

Jobs for February

❀ Water pot-grown azaleas regularly and thoroughly of you want to keep them for flowering next year. The peaty mixture they are grown in dries out easily and is difficult to re-wet.

❀ Cut away the old foliage of plants of *Epimedium* and the Lenten lily, *Helleborus corsicus.* This will allow you to see the flowers properly before the fresh new leaves are produced.

❀ Start begonia tubers into growth. Place them in trays or boxes of moist compost and water them sparingly until they begin to sprout. Keep them in good light once the shoots appear, to prevent them from becoming leggy.

❀ Prune late small-flowering clematis such as *C. tangutica* and *C. orientalis.* Cut the whole plant down to within three feet of the ground, the new growth made in spring and early summer will flower later in the year.

❀ Cut down canes of autumn-fruiting raspberries to within six inches of the ground.

❀ As daffodil and other spring bulbs come up, mark or make a note of areas where you would like to plant more. By the time autumn planting arrives you may have forgotten where the gaps in your existing plantings are.

❀ In dry weather clear any weeds from herbaceous and shrub borders. Time spent weeding now will save twice as much time later in the season .

❀ Give fruit trees and bushes a top dressing of well-rotted farmyard manure or garden compost.

❀ Plant new trees and shrubs only when the soil is not frozen or water-logged. After cold weather check that newly planted shrubs have not been lifted by the frost.

❀ Lift and divide snowdrops after they have finished flowering. Plants moved 'in the green' do much better than those planted as dry bulbs later in the year.

March

*By the end of March all our winter jobs must be finished, as
the Visitor Centre prepares to open for another year. The sheep
are rounded up from the meadow and return to Penrith until
the autumn; paths and steps are given a final sweeping, the
putting and croquet lawn is raked and scarified.
March weather is unpredictable; often it is wet and windy,
though it can be surprisingly mild. There are catkins on
willows, hazel and alders, the first spring bulbs appear and
shrubs such as rhododendrons, camellias, corylopsis and
ornamental currants begin to flower.*

Spring pruning

As the year turns gradually, and rather damply, from winter to
spring, there are several pruning jobs to be done in the garden. I
find them very satisfying, the finished result always looks neat
and tidy, and the plants in question are now ready to leap into
growth for another year. First on my list are the buddleias, whose
old flower heads have been left on through the winter as food for
the birds. They flower in mid to late summer, on wood produced
the same year, so they should be pruned hard back to a stubby
framework 1 to 2 feet high. Similarly, plants of the blue-flowered
Caryopteris x clandonensis and *Perovskia* 'Blue Spire' should be
pruned now. If left unpruned these shrubs will still bloom, but
they will soon become leggy with many non-flowering shoots
and the flowers will be smaller.

A second group of shrubs that should be pruned in early
spring are those with colourful stems that have provided us with
valuable colour throughout the winter. The dogwoods (*Cornus*
spp) and willows (*Salix* spp) are the most obvious candidates in
this group. Cut back to ground level, or stooled back to a main
trunk, the new shoots produced in spring and summer will
provide next winter's brightly coloured stems. If you are cutting
willow you may be able to find someone who makes willow

baskets, furniture or garden ornaments, who would be happy to take the cut wands off your hands. Again these plants can be left unpruned, they will eventually form large shrubs or in some cases small trees, the colours of the twigs and branches will be much duller and not so noticeable in winter.

Hydrangeas are often a problem when it comes to deciding when to prune. Although they can be pruned at any time during the winter, there is always a danger that new shoots may be damaged by frost, so they are traditionally pruned from early to mid spring. The old flower heads are cut back to a pair of buds just beneath, and about one third of the oldest stems are cut down to ground level. This opens up the bushes and encourages the growth of new shoots from the base. It is sometimes tempting to cut the whole thing right down, but this temptation is best resisted; hydrangeas flower on last year's wood, so cutting right back would mean a year with no flowers!

With all pruning, make sure you use a sharp pair of secateurs, making cuts just above a new bud or shoot. For larger cuts I use a pair of loppers or, better still, a small pruning saw, trying to avoid making ragged cuts which are slower to heal and may allow disease to enter.

Fruit and veg.

Some of our most attractive flowering plants are remarkably closely related to common-or-garden fruit and vegetables. Take the currants for example. Their genus, or plant group, *Ribes*, contains not only the well-known flowering currant (*Ribes sanguineum,*) but also the edible red and black currants (*Ribes rubrum* and *R. nigrum*) and the gooseberry (*Ribes uva-crispa*). A close look at the leaves and flowers will reveal some of the similarities that have persuaded botanists to group them together. I am fond of the regular variety of flowering currant, and grow several at Brockhole. 'Pulborough Scarlet' is a good colour form, having dark pink flowers with white centres, 'King Edward VII' is another good variety, with much darker flowers, 'Tydeman's White' has, unsurprisingly, white flowers! They are all early

flowerers, blooming almost as soon as the leaves appear in spring.

There are two other species of flowering currant that are worthy of attention. *Ribes laurifolium*, a native of China, flowers in late winter and early spring; its fat racemes of greenish-yellow flowers are most welcome as one of the first shrubs to flower each year. The leaves are evergreen, and the plant forms a squat, spreading bush. My parents-in-law have a good specimen,

Solanum crispum 'Glasnevin'

growing along the top of a garden wall so that the flowers appear to tumble down the brickwork. *Ribes speciosum* the fuchsia-flowered currant from North America, is another choice plant; we have grown it at Brockhole for many years and it always invites comments from visitors. The delicate bell-shaped flowers are produced in late spring and early summer, rich dark-red with protruding red stamens, they look just like tiny fuchsias. The bushes sport wicked spines and can reach a height and spread of up to 6 feet, although our plants have not grown this big.

The genus *Solanum* contains many common edible plants such as aubergines, peppers, tomatoes and potatoes, together with a smattering of poisonous weeds like the deadly nightshades. Away from the vegetable garden *Solanum crispum* 'Glasnevin' is a fast growing, semi-climbing shrub that looks marvellous growing up a south or west-facing wall where it enjoys the extra warmth and sunshine. The flowers appear in mid summer and last through until the first autumn frosts; they look like typical potato flowers, lilac-blue petals with prominent yellow anthers, supposedly scented though I have never been able to smell anything much! It must be remembered that although they resemble their edible cousins in many respects, some decorative solanaceous plants are toxic and should not be tasted or swallowed.

Rhododendrons

In parts of the country where the soils are acidic, as they are in the central Lake District, some of the most commonly grown shrubs are rhododendrons and azaleas. Many people are quite passionate about them, and many of the bigger gardens grow large and specialised collections. At this point I must hold up my hand and confess that when I came to Cumbria in 1987, I had no great liking for this particular group of plants. Their colours can be bright and garish, the foliage is often dark and dreary, and let's face it, after they have finished flowering in April and May, they can be remarkably dull for the other 10 months of the year.

Now, before the lynching party of rhododendron addicts

knocks at my door, let me add that over the last few years, much to my astonishment, rhododendrons have slowly begun to grow on me (not literally). I have discovered that there are hybrids such as 'Yellow Hammer', with small, canary-yellow blooms that flower from February to May and again in autumn. There are alpine varieties such as *R. camtschaticum*, which grow no more than 8-12 inches tall and have miniature creamy coloured flowers each spring. And there are the giants of the rhododendron world such as *R. sinogrande*, from Tibet and Burma, which can reach heights of 30 feet or more, making an ideal canopy for a woodland garden growing blue poppies, ferns, hellebores, hostas and other shade-loving plants.

Some species have the most beautiful 'indumentum', a covering of dense woolly, rusty-coloured hairs or scales on the underside of the leaves. To walk underneath a plant such as *R. falconeri*, and look up at the huge woolly leaves is quite a horticultural experience. Other species are blessed with the most amazing perfume; *R. luteum* has a scent that stops garden visitors in their tracks, looking for the source. There are species of rhododendron from almost every corner of the globe. A large specimen of *Rhododendron arboreum* has just come into flower at Brockhole, others like it will be flowering in Thailand, India and Sri Lanka. In a nearby bed are plants of *R. yunnanense* from China, and others hailing from Eastern Europe, Korea, Japan and North America. Many of the plants seen in gardens are hybrids, bred for special characteristics such as colour, shape and form. A particular favourite of mine is *R. 'Loderi King George'*; it has pale pink buds that open into huge trusses of scented, brilliant-white flowers.

Furry visitors

Whilst pruning a large orange-peel clematis on the kitchen garden trellis, I came across some wads of old, hairy seed heads tucked inside the mass of twiggy growths. At first I thought I had found one of last year's birds' nests, but on further investigation the wads turned out to be almost twelve inches across and several inches deep, much too large for the small birds that like to

Rhododendron arboreum

line their nests with soft clematis seeds. Instead, I now began to
suspect that this was the work of mice, but whether this was a
three-storey nest or simply a seed mountain for use in times of
food shortage I am still not sure. Of its makers there was, fortunately, no sign.

Mice have been a problem from time to time in the kitchen
garden. They like to eat the seeds of broad beans, climbing beans

and peas and have no qualms about digging them up and stealing them shortly after planting. I also suspect mice of nibbling at new seedlings as they emerge, but this may be due to the efforts of slugs. For several years now we have taken to germinating many of our vegetable seeds in the greenhouse or cold frame, planting them out only when most of the food store in the seed has been used up by the plant. Not that we haven't had problems with mice in the greenhouse too, but these are much easier to deal with than mice in the open, being easily caught using humane traps. One year we germinated several hundreds of acorns in the poly-tunnel, to grow into little oak trees for planting out in the Park. The mice had a field day! We had to resort to using benches with metal legs to prevent mice climbing onto the tables and stealing the acorns.

Mice are not the only furry pests in the gardens at Brockhole. The resident population of rabbits has been known to cause significant damage to plants in previous years, though at the moment we seem to be in a state of uneasy truce. There are some plants that they cannot resist, such as gentians and phlox. With these I have either given up trying to grow them (as with gentians) or we grow them in wire cages (as with phlox) that not only prevent rabbits nibbling the young shoots but also double up as plant supports later in the season. In general, I have found that rabbits prefer to eat freshly planted specimens, and we have found it useful to fence off newly planted areas for up to 18 months after planting. After this time the rabbits mostly ignore the new plants and if one or two do get nibbled, they are established enough to recover and start again. Trying to eradicate rabbits from the area completely seems to be a time-consuming and frustrating process, often resulting in an influx of next door's rabbits to fill the void created. Better to live with the rabbits you know perhaps?

Many people ask me if we are troubled by deer in the gardens. We see roe deer regularly and they have been known to do a little tree and shrub pruning for us, but we are not as badly plagued as some who live closer to open woodland or fell-side. Personally the novelty of having these large and elegant creatures wandering through the gardens has not yet worn off for me, and I am quite happy to sacrifice a few leaves and twigs for the privilege of watching deer at close quarters. That's not to say that I don't protect vulnerable new tree plantings with tree cages though; I'm not that fond of deer!

Conifers

Perhaps because of the great swathes of dreary spruce trees planted around the Lake District by various commercial forestry organisations, or the widely publicised problems of huge leyland cypress hedges, many people are reluctant to plant conifers in their gardens. This is unfortunate, as there are plenty of elegant and interesting conifers that can be used to great effect in both large and small plots. Conifers have several points in their favour. Firstly, they are evergreens, their leaves varying from the long, bundled needles of the pines, through the shorter needles of firs and junipers, to the scale-like leaves of the Monkey-Puzzle and the cypresses. Secondly, although only the yew, juniper and Scots pine are native to the British Isles, most other conifers come from the temperate regions of the world, and are generally hardy in British gardens. There are shapes, forms and colours to suit every situation, and the trees themselves are usually quite undemanding, growing in most soils apart from thin chalk, pure sand, or waterlogged conditions.

Here then are my top five conifers; no garden should be without at least one of these gems! First place goes to the Japanese umbrella pine, *Sciadopitys verticillata*. This is a slow-growing, conical tree with long needles arranged in whorls like the spokes of an umbrella. Second place goes to the good old Scots pine. I love its rusty-red bark and the way the trunks of older specimens split up and become flat topped with age. Third place to the cedars, *Cedrus libani, C. atlantica* and *C. deodara*. Few of us will not have taken the time to admire the spreading branches of a cedar of Lebanon on the lawn of some stately home. They do, however, need a great deal of space, and should not be planted in small gardens!

The swamp cypress, *Taxodium distichum*, is in fourth place. I have seen this growing in the Florida Everglades, where it defies the rule about not growing in waterlogged soils and flourishes in several inches of slowly moving water! It contradicts another general rule by being deciduous, its bright green feathery leaves turning a wonderful bronze-yellow before falling each autumn. The last of my favourites are the firs, and in particular the Colorado white fir, *Abies concolor*. The needles are bluish green and give the impression that the tree has been dusted with snow. Our tree at Brockhole is only about ten feet tall as yet, but it will eventually make a beautiful large tree with smooth grey bark.

British bulbs

Every year we gardeners plant thousands of exotic and hybridised bulbs in our gardens; tulips, daffodils, iris, grape-hyacinths, cyclamen, crocus and colchicum. Yet two types of bulbs that I derive just as much pleasure from are British natives, growing freely in woodlands and shady places and heralding the arrival of spring in great drifts of blue and white. They are of course bluebells and wood anemones, both of which enjoy the moist, leafy conditions provided in the hedgerows and woodlands of the Lake District. Both of them will also grow well in cultivation, and if conditions are right, they make excellent garden plants.

Anemone nemorosa, the wood anemone, is a small plant, with delicate white flowers and delicately divided leaves. It spreads by means of creeping rhizomes and will eventually form a thick ground cover, the leaves remaining attractive after the flowers have finished. There are several cultivated varieties, in shades of pink and blue, and a couple of double white varieties. Wood anemones can be a bit rampant if grown on the rock garden and are much better in a wild or woodland garden where the competition from tree and shrub roots keeps them under restraint. They also grow well in tubs or troughs, though these should be kept in the shade during the summer months after flowering has finished.

Bluebells have had so many Latin names over the last few years that I have lost track of their correct title! They too will grow almost anywhere in cool, moist, shady conditions and are a valuable plant for the semi-wild garden. In the formal garden they can be a nuisance, spreading rapidly, with leaves hanging around limply long after the flowers have finished. But in woodland and beneath shrubs they are unsurpassed for spring ground cover. Bluebells can appear with white flowers or in shades of pink and purple, though to my mind these are not as attractive as the original blue.

It is not easy to find either of these two plants for sale, though they are available through specialist bulb suppliers. Before buying any, always make sure that they have been propagated from garden plants and not taken from the wild. These are plants that need protecting in their wild habitats so that future generations can enjoy their spring displays as we do.

Erythroniums

With the welcome flowering of the daffodils each spring come the flowers of another favourite of mine; *Erythronium dens-canis*, the dog's-tooth violet. A native of Europe, this cheerful little plant grows each year from bulbs the shape of dogs' teeth. The leaves are 4 to 6 inches long, mid-green with a rich purple-brown marbling. The flowers, which are held above the leaves, can be white, pink or lilac, the six delicate petals curving gently backwards to reveal bluish-purple anthers! Each plant can bear up to 10 flowers and they seem happy to grow either in a shady woodland bed or out in the open in short grass.

A close relative of the dog's-tooth violet that has made itself quite at home at Brockhole is the American trout lily, *Erythronium revolutum*. I grew it originally from seed given to me by a friend who is an Alpine plant enthusiast. Although I was dubious of my ability to germinate such an exotic sounding plant, a whole tray full of trout lilies sprouted, not unlike the proverbial mustard and cress, in the cold frame the following spring. They stayed in this tray for a couple of years, being too tiny to plant out individually, until they were eventually planted into a shady position in the garden. From there, they have gone from strength to strength, and during the last couple of years they have begun to seed themselves around the bed, making a shoal of trout lilies! The leaves are longer and paler than the dog's-tooth violets but they have the same attractive marbling. The flowers are held 8 to 10 inches above the foliage; they are lilac-pink with yellow anthers.

The third erythronium that grows at Brockhole is a cultivated variety, *Erythronium* 'Pagoda'. This is a much beefier plant than the other two, although it has shown no inclination to spread any further than the original clump that I planted several years ago. Its sulphur-yellow flowers are held up to 12 inches above the bronze-green foliage. The petals are curved backwards like the roof of a Chinese pagoda, to reveal deeper yellow anthers. I have planted it at the base of a holly hedge, which with hind sight may be slightly too dry a spot. On the other hand, it does keep coming up year after year and the sharp holly leaves beneath the hedge may be deterring slug attack, so I am reluctant to move it.

These are plants of the deciduous woodlands and mountain meadows of Europe, Asia and North America, and they are best grown in light shade, in humus rich soil. An annual top dressing of compost or leaf mould can be beneficial, but otherwise they do not need a rich soil or any other fertiliser. The bulbs do not like to dry out and they should be planted at least 4 inches deep. Dormant bulbs can be planted in autumn, existing plants may be split and transplanted "in the green" as they come into growth, as long as they are watered in well.

Jobs for March

❀ If conditions are suitable, lawns will benefit from a good raking to remove thatch and moss. Very wet areas can be spiked with a garden fork; improve drainage further by brushing in a top dressing of sand or loam.

❀ Finish any tree and shrub planting this month. Any planted later will need much more aftercare watering than those planted before the end of March.

❀ Prune gooseberries and redcurrants.

❀ Prune buddleias by cutting back hard to a low framework of stout stems about a foot high. The plants will flower in late summer, on wood produced this spring. Cut hardy fuchsias down to ground level, they too will flower on the new wood in late summer.

❀ Lift and divide any herbaceous perennials that have got too big or that have started to die out in the centre. Replant smaller clumps after enriching the soil with garden compost or manure.

❀ Finish any winter construction jobs such as paving or fencing, before the regular work of mowing and weeding begins in April.

❀ Prune established shrubs such as aucuba, laurel, witch hazel and willows. Cut out completely any diseased, crossing or badly shaped branches, then remove up to one third of the oldest branches to ground level, leaving an open and healthy framework.

❀ Repot foliage plants and ferns as they begin to come into growth.

❀ Sow seeds of herbaceous perennials, herbs and alpines in a cold frame or unheated glasshouse.

❀ Prune hybrid tea and floribunda roses if they were not done in the autumn.

April

April is a contrary month in the Lake District; the days can be warm and beautifully sunny, with temperatures into double figures (centigrade), whilst night temperatures reach as low as -2C or -4C, with sharp overnight frosts that can damage the blooms of rhododendrons, camellias and magnolias. The garden can be bathed in warm sunshine whilst the fell tops are covered in a sparkling layer of snow. It can be snowing, sleeting, hailing or just plain raining for days on end, though my recollection is that April is one of our drier months, together with May, September and October.

Late frosts

A few warm days and, suddenly, spring flowers are appearing like magic all over the garden. I love this time of year, with all the fresh promise of a brand new growing season ahead. I take a slow walk round the beds and borders each evening before going home, trying to keep track of what has come up and what has come into flower over the last few days.

Along with some fine spring weather this month often gives us some not-so-fine sleet, snow and, worst of all from a plant's point of view, frost. Several rhododendrons, magnolias and camellias in the gardens at Brockhole are prone to having their blooms spoilt by the frost; those protected by walls or in sheltered spots mostly escape but exposed plants and those which catch the early morning sun do not fare so well. The damage that upsets me most is that to plants of *Pieris*. Here it is not blossom that is damaged but the bright red, tender new shoots, just starting to emerge. These become brown and shrivelled when caught by the frost, and although the shrubs will recover they will have received a significant setback in their growth.

Frosted shoots of *Pieris* should be cut back to undamaged buds as soon as possible. If you have the time, it might be worth removing damaged blossoms from rhododendrons and magno-

The Orangery at Brockhole

lias. Some magnolias will flower again, in a more limited way, in the autumn but for the rest we will have to wait another year for more perfect blooms. If you are planting camellias it is a good idea to choose those from the williamsii group rather than the more common *Camellia japonica* hybrids. The flowers of *Camellia x williamsii* drop off the plant if they are frosted, so that any still in bud will have a chance to open and look good without being surrounded by damaged blooms. Those of us who are really organised and watch the weather forecasts carefully can protect plants like *Pieris* from frost damage, covering them overnight with a piece of horticultural fleece or some light material such as old net curtains, to keep the frost from touching the leaves. This is remarkably successful, though it takes some skill to drape material over the whole of a large bush without breaking the fragile shoots!

Some newly emerging herbaceous plants may be damaged by the frosty nights, here there is little to be done except wait for them to start again. Established perennials have sturdy root systems that are not affected by the cold and they will send up new shoots as soon as the weather warms up again.

Bedding plants are a different matter altogether. The garden centres and nurseries are brimming with them by April, tempting us to buy our summer bedding and to get cracking with summer planting schemes. But beware! These plants are generally not frost-hardy and should not be planted out until all danger of frost has passed. So if you don't have a greenhouse or a conservatory, hold back for a few weeks or you could have to do your summer planting twice! If you buy bedding plants from an indoor nursery area, remember to harden them off before planting them out in the open. This means exposing them to increasing amounts of cooler weather before final planting, perhaps by standing them out on mild nights, putting them in a cold frame, or turning down the heating in the greenhouse, and leaving the windows open on milder nights.

Seed sowing

The arrival of the seed-sowing season is always an exciting time in the gardeners' calendar year. A glance at the back of at least 75% of seed packets will reveal the magic words "Sowing – March to May" and many of us cannot wait to get started! It may be the thought of all that cunningly stored energy, just waiting for the trigger to burst into life; or it may be the promise of a fresh start and a new growing season, with all last year's failures and frustrations forgotten. Whatever the reason, I have always been fascinated by the process of sowing seeds, and for me it is the signal that the next gardening year has truly begun.

Few gardening jobs can be quite as satisfying as the process of sowing seeds. Take some wide, shallow pots, fill with fine seed compost to within half an inch of the rim, firm it down gently, and then scatter the seeds thinly and evenly onto the surface. Cover with a thin layer of compost, preferably shaken through a fine sieve (to produce a really smooth surface with no obstacles to divert the emerging seedlings.) A gentle watering with a fine spray is the equivalent of lighting the blue touch-paper, all that is needed now is to place the pots somewhere warm and to wait patiently for the seeds to germinate.

A couple of years ago I discovered what many growers have

The house and pergola, with wisteria flowering

obviously known for centuries (I can be a bit slow on the uptake!) The alternative to waiting patiently for seeds to germinate is to apply some bottom heat! Pots of seeds placed in a propagator, with soil warming cables beneath the pots, will not only germinate in less than half the time of pots left on the greenhouse staging. They will also germinate much more evenly, so that the resulting seedlings are all ready to prick out at the same time. We had been using our small propagator simply for rooting cuttings; now, at this time of the year, the cuttings have to battle for space with pots of germinating seeds. Fortunately, the turnover rate is quite rapid so there is generally room for all.

It is important to remember that seedlings raised in a propagator have been cosseted, and they may receive a check in growth if they are not weaned off it carefully. Only remove seedlings from the case on mild, bright days, and try to keep them in the warmest part of the greenhouse until they are properly acclimatised. If you are germinating seeds in the house, it is possible to hurry them along by putting them close to a radiator or boiler (not too close or the heat may be too much.) The atmosphere indoors is generally much drier than in a greenhouse and the pots will need covering with a polythene bag to prevent them drying out too quickly.

Many seeds germinate better in the dark, and the pots may be covered with a sheet of newspaper. All pots of seeds, wherever they are, should be checked daily and kept moistened with a fine-rosed watering can. Immediately the seedlings start to emerge, any polythene or paper should be removed and the seedlings placed in a light, airy position preferably away from too much direct sunlight. Slightly cooler temperatures now will produce sturdier seedlings that will be ready to pot up as soon as the first true leaves start to appear.

Problems in the greenhouse

A bench full of seedlings, newly rooted cuttings and sprouting tubers must be a tempting sight to the host of pests and diseases that begin to show themselves in the greenhouse at this time of year. Good housekeeping, regular cleaning, tidying and disinfecting will keep them at bay for a fair while but there are always some plants that will succumb before it is time for them to be planted out.

The fungal diseases that attack emerging seedlings are one of my pet hates; one day you have a pot full of happily germinating seedlings, the next day half of them have collapsed and died, to be followed by the rest not long after! Damping off is generally caused by a fungus called *Rhizoctonia*, which attacks the base of the seedlings, causing them to soften and collapse. It can be treated successfully with various chemicals but there are some useful preventative measures that can be taken to discourage it from taking hold in the first place.

As mentioned above, a clean, tidy greenhouse is a good starting point, together with the use of clean, preferably disinfected pots and seed trays. Air movement and circulation are also important; although it is not usually practical to heat a greenhouse whilst leaving the windows slightly open, a similar effect can be achieved by running a fan heater, on cold setting, pushing the air around and preventing it from becoming still and

Views of Brockhole, clockwise from top: the main house; young monkey-puzzle, *Araucaria araucana*; the house and top terrace.

The phlox border in late summer *(Graham Beech)*

The Orangery at Brockhole

The Temperate House, Royal Botanic Gardens,
Kew; right – *Protea obtusifolia* flowering in the
Temperate House.

Spring bedding: white tulips and mixed wallflowers

Tulips flowering in the box-edged L-shaped beds

stagnant. Opening windows and doors on fine, sunny days, even for just an hour or so, will help to freshen things up.

Sterile seed compost is a great help, any fungal spores in the compost should have been destroyed by the sterilising process. Do remember though, not to leave opened bags of compost in the greenhouse where spores can sneak in ready to attack any new sowings. Store compost in a cool, dry place, with the bag closed as tightly as possible, only bring it into the greenhouse when you are ready to use it. Sow seeds thinly in their pots and trays; overcrowding of germinating seedlings is one of the commonest causes of damping off. If you need a lot of the same plants it is much better to sow more than one trayful, with plenty of room for each seedling, than it is to sow them thickly all in one pot.

Watering is important in the control of damping off and many other greenhouse diseases. The key is not to allow pots to become waterlogged; let them almost dry out before watering, then give them a good soaking. Do not be tempted to water "little and often" as the surface dries out – the bottom of the pot will still be wet. Better to wait another day or two and then give a more thorough watering to wet the whole pot. If, like me, you habitually over-water, try to use shallow pots or trays rather than full sized pots, this reduces the amount of waterlogging possible! If any pots or trays do become infected, remove them from the greenhouse as soon as possible. Put seedlings and compost in the bin rather than on the compost heap, and disinfect the containers with Jeyes Fluid before using them again.

Finally, do make sure that fungus is the real problem behind your collapsing seedlings. I spent a lot of time with fungicides one year, cursing damping off for blighting my seedlings and trying unsuccessfully to wipe it out, only to discover that the true villain was something completely different. We had an infestation of springtails, tiny whitish pests only just visible to the naked eye, that were eating the seedling roots and causing them to topple over. A couple of applications of insecticide were all that was needed to clear up the problem!

Vegetable growing

With the relatively low cost of vegetables in our supermarkets, and the wide range available from all parts of the globe, you

might be forgiven for concluding that growing your own vegetables at home was a waste of time and energy. The best argument for growing your own used to be that the produce was fresh and could be grown organically. Now, even organic vegetables are widely available in the shops, and freshness is demanded by all customers, so why waste valuable flower-growing space on growing common or garden vegetables?

At Brockhole we have struggled with this problem for some time. We have a small kitchen garden that produces a relatively small amount of organically grown soft fruit, herbs and vegetables; not nearly enough quantity to supply our café, and although the quality is generally good we cannot guarantee the cooks a steady supply of home grown fruit and veg. So we have decided to go for a three-part strategy.

Part one consists of growing salad crops and garnishing plants, that are quite expensive to buy, that are needed by the café in relatively small amounts and that are best eaten extra-fresh, picked straight from the garden. Part one candidates include parsley, borage, endive, dill, chives, red and green "Salad Bowl" lettuce, rocket, and radicchio, a variety of red chicory that looks and tastes great in autumn salads, having crispy red hearts like lettuce.

Part two of the great vegetable plot has an educational angle to it. We will be growing a collection of around 15 varieties of plants that combine extra good nutritional value with special properties that can help combat many common and major diseases. Having force-fed my son a satsuma a day for the whole of one winter, and having been rewarded by a complete lack of colds and flu bugs, I am now a firm believer in the protective value of certain foods!

So our plot will include artichokes, purple-sprouting broccoli and calabrese, cabbage, carrots, onions and garlic, two varieties of lettuce, red-stemmed chard, chicory and sorrel. Our list also includes chillies and sunflowers that will be grown in other parts of the garden.

Part three is a very exclusive category that consists of vegetables that are enormous fun to grow and that are still expensive to buy in the shops. There is only one candidate, somewhat frowned upon by certain of the gardeners but a great favourite of the Head Gardener, so bound to be grown. It is of course that king of vegetables, the pumpkin! it takes up masses of valuable space and tastes revolting, but it makes superb pumpkin lanterns for Halloween. For me it is the epitome of why we should continue to grow our own vegetables in spite of all the sensible arguments against the practice; it is one of the most enjoyable, peaceful and satisfying occupations that remains in this age of computers and hi-tech entertainment!

Container gardening

April is the time to be planning ideas for pots and containers to give a summer long display of colour; whether your garden is large, small or just a doorstep or window-box, it will look better and brighter with a potful of plants.

Almost anything will make a container – old buckets, watering cans, baskets, it is not necessary to spend a lot of money – some of the most original displays have 'home made' planters. Many garden centres, nurseries and DIY stores are doing special offers at this time of year, and there is a huge range of terracotta pots, glazed pots, urns, tubs and other containers to choose from. Generally it is best to choose the biggest pots you can afford, as smaller pots not only hold fewer plants, they also require more frequent watering. Drainage is important, so ensure there are some holes in the bottom to allow excess water to drain out. If you want to keep your pots outside all year, check that they are marked 'frost-proof', or they will crack and split in cold weather.

Traditionally, gardeners have preferred to use loam-based or John Innes type of compost for containers; it dries out quite slowly and its weight prevents top heavy displays from falling over in windy weather, or when pushed by the dog! However, soil-less compost will work just as well, and less weight means that the pots are easier to carry and move around the garden. If you are conservation minded, choose a peat-free compost; at Brockhole we use a coir-based potting compost mixed with a little grit and charcoal.

Whatever medium you use, it will benefit from the addition of

some slow-release fertiliser granules. If you are not able to water very often, some water-retaining gel such as Broadleaf P4 or Swellgel may be useful, but make sure you soak the granules well before mixing them with the compost. The first time I tried them, I mixed them into the compost dry and then potted up my plants with the mixture. Overnight the gel expanded, soaking up all the water in the pots and raising my plants four inches above the top of the pots! I am still trying to live it down in the face of much ribbing from the other gardeners.

You could probably grow almost anything in a pot if you tried hard enough – from trees to vegetables, from alpines to palms. Some of the most successful summer displays consist of mixtures of annuals and half-hardy or tender perennials; you can grow your own from seed and cuttings, or start with small pots from a nursery or garden centre. (Do remember not to put these plants outside without protection until the last frosts have gone)

It's a good idea to aim for one or two taller plants in the centre of your display, medium sized plants in most of the container, with trailing or floppier plants around the edge. Good, strong, tall plants include the blue or red salvias, argyranthemums (marguerites), tall white nicotianas and fuchsias. A more tropical effect can be achieved by using cannas, abutilon or daturas (angel's trumpet). We have grown castor-oil plants (*Ricinis communis*) for several years now – it's quite a striking effect. You could also use shrubby plants such as phormiums (New Zealand flax), eucalyptus or bamboo. Some of my favourite 'middle ground' plants are the purple heliotrope, verbena, white and red geraniums, petunias, pink *Diascia*, *Osteospermum* and the smaller green and maroon nicotianas. The best trailing plants include lobelias, *Helichrysum petiolare* and the yellow flowered *Bidens aurea*. Tuck in some nasturtium seeds to fill any gaps and in true hanging basket tradition fit as many plants into each container as you can.

A pot containing just one species or variety of plant can be very attractive – try all begonias, or all petunias, geraniums, or blue and white *Salvia farinacea*. For those who prefer the simple touch there are many garden plants that will grow happily in pots year after year, with only a minimal amount of care. Hostas look particularly good, as do ferns. I have also tried geraniums, *Alchemilla*, lilies, foxgloves and *Onopordum* (giant thistles) with great success. Small shrubs can look great on their own in pots, you might like to try a bay tree, holly or clipped box, small-leaved maples, camellias or *Nerium* (oleander) to give a Mediterranean feel to your patio.

Plants in pots have three basic needs: light, water and food. Place your containers according to what you have planted; flowering plants like a bright sunny position, garden plants and shrubs can cope with less sunny or shady spots, while plants such as hostas, ferns and ivies (especially the variegated sorts) can be used to brighten up the darker corners. Water is the most important requirement; while pots should not be over-watered and soggy, it is usually lack of water that results in a disappointing display. Better to water thoroughly at least twice a week (daily in hot, dry weather) than 'little and often'. Small amounts of water will only wet the top few inches, leaving the rest bone dry. So, water generously from the top until water runs out through the drainage holes, or stand your pot in a dish of water and let it soak up from the base until all the compost is moist. A mulch of chopped bark, pebbles or gravel will help prevent water loss through evaporation.

Even if you have added slow-release fertiliser to your compost, the plants will benefit from a weekly feed; a good tip is to use liquefied seaweed or tomato fertiliser rich in phosphates to encourage flowering. Regular deadheading will help to keep plants looking at their best, and don't forget to ask a friend to water them for you if you are away on holiday.

Plant names

Latin names for plants often appear cumbersome and difficult to pronounce. They can be tricky to remember and an English or common name seems at first glance to be a much easier option. Far simpler, you will say, to talk about bluebells than *Hyacinthoides non-scriptus*. But, I will reply, if you talked of bluebells with someone from Scotland, they would probably be referring to *Campanula rotundifolia*, a plant that you and I would call a harebell. Confused? Read on ....

Not only may the same common name apply to different plants, but a single plant may have several different common names. *Gallium aparine* is not only goosegrass, but also cleavers and sticky Willie. Common names can change over the years, they can go out of fashion or disappear completely. Or a plant may have no English common name at all because it comes from another country or because it is a hybrid between two other plants. Gardening books are sometimes not above inventing common names for such plants to make for easier reading!

In contrast to all this confusion, the Latin name of a plant applies to only one individual plant and no other, and this name is the same in Scotland, France, Japan and everywhere else in the world. Latin names may be difficult to pronounce but they are very precise and leave no room for confusion of any kind.

The name is in two parts, first the genus, then the species. Closely related plants will share the same genus, with different species names to tell them apart, for example *Rosa canina* and *Rosa glauca* are both species of rose. Latin names can often tell us quite a lot about the nature of plants, for example their colour; species names are often colour related – purpurea means purple, nigra means black, coccinea means red and variegata is variegated!

Other names hint at the country of origin of the plant; *Acer japonica, Rosa virginiana, Actinidia chinensis.* Yet other names tell of the plant explorer who discovered them, or the botanist who named them; *Rosa banksiae* is named after Sir Joseph Banks, *Viburnum farreri* was discovered by Reginald Farrer and the genus *Fuchsia* is named after Leonhart Fuchs.

Plants with scented or smelly flowers may have species names such as *odorata* or *foetidissima,* or the name may tell of the size and shape of the leaves or flowers; *microphyllos* means tiny leaves, *macropetala* means big petals and *arborescens* means tree-like. Hybrids are indicated by 'x' – for example *Rosa x odorata* is a hybrid between *Rosa chinensis* and *Rosa gigantea.*

Jobs for April

❀ Give the lawn a first cut when conditions are dry enough. Set the blades fairly high and aim for a light topping rather than anything too severe.

❀ Sow grass seed from the beginning of the month onwards.

❀ Cut down plants of *Cornus* or dogwood to within a few inches of the ground. The bright new stems produced this summer will provide valuable colour for the winter months.

❀ If the weather is mild sow seeds of hardy annuals directly into the soil where they are to flower. Sow them in short rows to make them easy to spot amongst any weed seedlings that emerge at the same time.

❀ Mulch beds and borders with a thick layer of garden compost, rotted manure or bark to reduce summer weeding and water loss.

❀ Begin to stake early-flowering herbaceous perennials, such as peonies, that usually flop over. Use hazel twigs, garden canes or proprietary plant supports.

❀ Cut the flower heads of daffodils and tulips after they have finished flowering, to prevent them from putting energy into seed production. Do not cut the foliage down until it begins to yellow and die.

❀ Sharpen up the edges of lawns with a spade or half-moon cutter. This will make clipping the edges less of a chore during the summer.

❀ Prune forsythias after they have finished flowering, cutting one third of the stems down to ground level.

❀ Sow parsley, in the garden or in pots to stand by the kitchen door.

May

During May the atmosphere in the garden gradually changes. The brilliant fresh green leaves of trees and hedges mature to deeper shades whilst the flowering bulbs and delicate early flowers begin to give way to the more robust herbaceous flowers of summer. The gardens seem to be alive with birdsong; summer visitors – flycatchers, willow warblers, chiff-chaffs and blackcaps, swell the ranks of our resident birds.

The May bank holidays can be busy times in the gardens at Brockhole, especially if the weather is sunny as it often is in this month. We generally have one day in May when we open for the National Garden Scheme, the gardeners take guided walks around the grounds, there are plants for sale and other plant-orientated events laid on for visitors to the Centre.

Flowering trees

Everywhere you look there are trees and shrubs in flower: rhododendrons, azaleas, brooms, gorse, magnolias, berberis, hawthorns, crab apples, cherries, wisteria, spireas, the list goes on. In general, I favour those with softer, subtler colours; more a pale yellow, *Rhododendron lutescens* person than a bright pink or orange, hybrid Azalea person, if you see what I mean. But there is one very brightly coloured tree, flowering each May at Brockhole, which breaks this rule. It is the Chilean firebush, *Embothrium coccineum*, its flowers are the most brilliant orange-red, and I think it's wonderful!

As its common name suggests the *Embothrium* comes from South America; it belongs to the Proteaceae family along with those amazing South African proteas that the more exclusive flower arrangers like to use. It makes a small to medium sized tree, liable to suckering, with deep green, lance-shaped leaves. The flowers are its crowning glory, each one a fairly small, tubular construction joined to a group of others in a dense raceme. The overall effect is a wonderful deep orange glow that lights up the garden from late spring to early summer each year.

The Chilean firebush is generally frost-hardy, though it does need planting in a sheltered position away from cold winds. It prefers a lime-free soil, with plenty of moisture, otherwise it requires very little attention at all in exchange for this spectacular floral show.

The larger, more common trees are also flowering now and should not be overlooked when it comes to appreciating spring blossom. I can still remember discovering, at the age of nineteen, that "normal" trees like oak, ash and sycamore had flowers too! Some of the ornamental maples have very elegant flowers, complimenting the fresh bright colours of the new foliage. Other interesting flowering trees worth looking out for on your travels include the flowering dogwood, *Cornus kousa*, the snowdrop tree, *Halesia monticola*, and the Judas tree, *Cercis siliquastrum*.

Every year I hope that our tulip tree will at last be mature enough to flower. Planted by the previous Head Gardener, it must be at least 20 years old. Tulip tree flowers are just as their name describes, like greenish-white tulip flowers, with orange markings. The leaves are a little like tulips in shape too; large and flat with a deeply notched tip and lobed sides. But beware of planting it in a small garden or in a confined space! If you want to see mature tulip trees, there are two growing on the lakeside at Waterhead and they are huge. Come to think of it, I can't remember seeing these flowering either, so perhaps I'm in for a long wait with our young tree!

Companionable planting

Nature is a dab hand at mixing wild plants up together so that each one compliments its companions. Take bluebells, pink campion and white stitchwort for example, each of them is good to look at in its own right, but mix them up together and they look wonderful. The same can be true of garden plants; most often it seems to happen by accident, but occasionally, contrived plantings can achieve one of those mixtures that enhance the beauty of both plants well beyond the sum of the two individuals.

An early flowering clematis, *C. macropetala*, and a normally half-hardy climber, *Eccremocarpus scaber*, both come into

flower together at Brockhole in early May. I like the clematis anyway, but the *Eccremocarpus* is a rather virulent shade of rosy-pink. Together however they look extremely classy and I have been tempted to take one of those cameo photos that look so good in the gardening magazines. To cap it all the *Eccremocarpus* carries on flowering until the autumn, its bright flowers given a subtlety it does not deserve by the feathery seed heads of the fruiting clematis.

Once you start looking, there are examples of this kind of planting all over the place. In my front garden at home, a common or garden purple aubretia has made itself wildly attractive simply by growing up to and through a clump of the black grass *Ophiopogon planiscapus* 'Nigrescens'. Pink and white old-fashioned roses with the soft grey of lavender and catmint, wallflowers with tulips growing up through them and montbretia mixed with alchemilla are some good examples of companionable plantings, all the better for growing together rather than side by side. Sometimes the enhancement only lasts a few days, or even hours, until one or other of the plants changes or goes over. In a neighbour's garden a great drift of variegated periwinkle joins forces with a large clump of white arabis. Whilst both are just emerging in early spring they look great together; once they are at their full heights they just look overcrowded!

Self-seeding plants such as aquilegias and foxgloves, have a habit of planting themselves in places the gardener would not have chosen, and often look quite fetching, so it pays to leave a few self-sown plants in place to see how they will look in flower. Bulbs such as lilies, alliums and snowdrops, which can be tucked in between other plantings, make excellent companion plants, as do the closely packed plants in a pot or hanging basket.

Old-fashioned roses

The swifts that nest in our house roof arrive in May each year for the summer season. Like the trendiest guests at parties, they always arrive after the swallows and housemartins, and they are always the first to leave. For a few short months they swoop round the house at breakneck speed, filling the air with their screaming cries; I wait for them to arrive each year and when they have gone I miss them.

There are plants like this too, not the 'good value' sort that flower for long periods and can be relied upon to provide colour in the garden for months at a time, but those that appear abruptly, flower all too briefly and then are gone for another year. Old-fashioned and shrub roses are like this, the swifts of the rose world. Modern, hybrid tea and floribunda roses come into the 'good value' category, flowering reliably, often from March right through to Christmas. The older roses, on the other hand, come into bloom in late spring and most have finished flowering by the middle of summer.

These old-fashioned varieties and species of rose do have several advantages over their modern cousins. They are much tougher for instance, suffering from fewer pests and diseases, and are longer lived, lasting often for decades. They require little in the way of pruning, merely a little thinning from time to time, with the removal of any weak or dead wood. The flowers have a charm and subtlety of shape and colour that modern roses have lost somewhere along the way. Best of all is their perfume; nearly

Old-fashioned roses

all of them have a strong, delicious fragrance that can fill the garden on a still day, almost like someone taking the lid off a scent bottle.

The short flowering period may seem like a disadvantage, but it certainly makes me appreciate the flowers all the more whilst they are there. Amongst my favourites are the Gallica roses, the oldest of all garden roses, including *Rosa* 'Mundi' that is striped crimson and white like toothpaste! Then there are the moss roses, such as 'William Lobb' and 'Blanche Moreau', which have sepals covered with a soft, moss-like growth; and the rugosa roses, many of which will flower for a second time in late summer. The best rugosa we have at Brockhole is called 'Agnes', with wonderfully fragrant, double, amber-yellow flowers. The flowers of the wild or species roses, like *Rosa glauca* and *Rosa moyesii*, are often small and simple; best appreciated for their massed effect, they have the added bonus of colourful and decorative hips to follow in the autumn.

Saving water

When I wrote this article, sitting on a bench in the back yard of our Cockermouth home, the weather had been fine for just over a week. It was soon raining again, but already there had been an item by the water company in our local paper asking us to use less water in case of shortages in summer! This could be taken as an insult, since we poor residents of Cumbria seem to spend at least 11 months of the year in our wellies and waterproofs. But politics aside, there are several sound reasons why we should spend less time watering in the garden. The first is that watering is time-consuming and not very interesting, how much nicer to be sitting in a deck chair reading the paper or just enjoying the flowers. Secondly, if you have a water meter installed, irrigation of any kind can be expensive. Finally, and most importantly, applying extra water to plants grown in the open ground may not actually be very good for them!

Newly planted bedding needs a good watering-in, but thereafter, unless the plants are wilting badly, it is best to let the roots grow downwards in search of their own water supply. Unless you are able to literally soak the ground every time you water, a light sprinkling will only wet the top few inches of the soil. The plant roots will stay in this top layer and remain weak and shallow. Herbaceous plants and established trees and shrubs are well able to cope with a bit of dry weather. Their roots should be well down into damp soil, and anything you add to the top layer will simply evaporate and be of no use to the plants. Newly planted trees and shrubs do need to be watered regularly, and here it is a case of a good drink every few days being much better than a sip of water every day. Again, the idea is to encourage the new roots to grow downwards rather than towards the surface in search of water.

The key to conserving the water already in the soil is to apply a mulch to the surface. A typical mulch is simply a barrier between the moist soil below and the dry air above. It can be anything from a layer of organic material like bark chippings, to an inorganic layer of pebbles or an old carpet. The simplest of mulches is a layer of finely hoed soil, free of weeds that will compete with your plants for moisture. The layer of fine soil breaks the capillary link with the soil beneath, water does not easily travel upwards between the soil crumbs. So whilst the surface looks dry and dusty, a couple of inches below the soil is still moist. The best mulches, such as manure or garden compost, contain some plant food but this is not essential; mulches containing nutrients are best applied in spring, winter rains will leach out the goodness before the plants begin to grow. Grass clippings make a good if rather unsightly mulch; don't put them too high up the stems of plants though, as they can heat up and damage delicate bark.

Plants grown in pots must be watered regularly of course. They have no link with the ground water and must rely on what you give them. Here again a generous soaking every few days is much better than a little bit every day. Try to water early in the morning or in the evening to allow the water time to sink down through the pot, or stand the pot in a tray of water and allow it time to soak upwards. Mulch the top of the pot with gravel or pebbles to reduce evaporation from the soil surface.

So much for using less water, what about collecting more of it? Installing a water butt on a convenient downpipe can collect an impressive amount of water in a very short space of time; and then you can use as much as you like!

Plants or weeds?

When is a weed not a weed? Answer: when it's a garden plant! There are several garden plants around that are cultivated varieties of pernicious weeds and that garden centres and nurseries are encouraging us to grow in our gardens. Some of these plants are perfectly innocent, but some are not...

Take for example the variety of common celandine we have been growing at Brockhole for at least eight years now. Unlike normal celandine, which would have spread to cover a large area if left undisturbed for that length of time, *Ranunculus ficaria* 'Brazen Hussy' has merely fattened up to make a handsome clump. It has bright yellow spring flowers that contrast brilliantly with the deep bronze foliage, and is well worth a place in anyone's garden. At the other extreme, I recently saw for sale a variegated variety of the common ground elder. It looked like a fairly respectable plant safely in its pot, delicately divided green and white leaves, low growing, ideal as ground cover. Then I spotted it growing in a nearby display bed, and it was showing all the characteristics of its plain green sibling; spreading rapidly and smothering nearby plants, undoubtedly twining its fleshy white roots inextricably through theirs.

There are now cultivated varieties of many common weeds and wildflowers; cow parsley, with pink flowers or variegated leaves, double-flowered buttercups and varieties of plantains, bistort, daisies and foxgloves. There is even a white-flowered variety of willow-herb that will seed itself freely throughout the garden!

The point of all this is that many of these plants are attractive and could be useful additions to the garden. Imagine mixing the variegated ground elder with existing ground elder instead of trying to weed it out. White willow-herb in a wildflower area would be lovely, as would pink cow parsley. In the right place, where they will not spread or seed uncontrollably into formal beds and borders these could be great plants. But think carefully before planting them and try to see them growing in someone else's garden before risking your own. I foolishly failed to follow this advice when I planted a small potful of a pretty, purple-leaved variety of yellow loosestife in one of our borders. It came up in great swathes, threatening to swamp the rest of the more delicate plants in the bed! Time for some careful weeding, and the removal of the culprit to a less sensitive area.

Television gardening

People occasionally ask me if, as a professional gardener, I watch gardening programmes on television. They are often quite surprised when I answer that I do. "Are they any good?" is usually the next question. Well, some are and some aren't in my opinion. Sensible, down to earth (excuse the pun) shows like "Gardeners' World" have a wealth of information, presented in an informative way, usually without talking down to the viewer. The range of plants shown is generally good and these programmes are valuable for giving tips and ideas for what you could be doing in your own garden. If I have any criticisms it's that some techniques and procedures are glossed over quite quickly, when more detail might have been appropriate, and that they do not always draw attention to environmentally sensitive products like peat-free compost and chemical alternatives.

Question number three: "What about these garden 'make over' programmes?" Now I really am in two minds over these. I like the ones where the owners do a lot of the work, it shows people that they can have a go at renovating their gardens without being scared of making mistakes. And I like it when the amounts of money spent on plants and materials are listed. Why is it that people are quite happy to spend several hundred pounds on decorating and refurbishing a room in their house, but are reluctant to spend more than a few bob on their gardens? I also like it when the cameras revisit the new gardens at a later date, to see how practical they really were.

On the other hand, I have never seen the fees of the designer or the professional gardeners and builders costed out. Owners should expect to pay between £15 and £30 an hour for a garden designer's time, and if you think that's unreasonable just look at your last garage bill and ask whether your mechanic has spent more time training and gaining experience than the designer. With gardeners, I'm quite sure that you get what you pay for. It is perfectly possible to pay the minimum wage for a jobbing gardener, but if you want someone who knows how to look after plants properly you should be prepared to spend at least £12 per hour for a qualified professional.

Finally, I am sick of the sight of decking, and a lot of the gardens seem to have more to do with showing off the wacky ideas of trendy presenters than creating a garden that fits in well with its surround-ings. But that won't stop me watching; it's important to know what the opposition is up to even if you don't agree with them!

Dryopteris wallichiana

Jobs for May

❀ Plant water lilies and other aquatic plants. Lift and split any large or overcrowded pond plants.

❀ Clip over lavender bushes after they have begun to shoot, cutting right down to the old wood. This should prevent them becoming too woody and dying out in the centre.

❀ Lower the height of mower blades after the third or fourth cut. Do not cut too low all at once, little and often is the best policy.

❀ Clear out spring bedding as it begins to go over. Fork over the soil and work in some organic material, leaving it to rest for a few days before planting out summer bedding.

❀ If you have a greenhouse, conservatory or garden room, plant up hanging baskets in early May for a head start. Keep them indoors at night until the end of the month.

❀ Thin out seedlings of annuals and vegetables sowed last month.

❀ Clip box hedges.

❀ Lift tulips after the foliage has died down, put the bulbs in an airy place to dry out. Clean all the soil off them and store in a cool, dark, dry place until autumn.

❀ Apply shade paint to greenhouses and frames if they are getting too hot in sunny weather.

❀ Do not be tempted to plant out summer bedding or tender vegetables until the risk of late frosts has passed. This may not be until the last week in May or the first week in June.

June

In June the garden seems to be full of scents; the perfumes from old-fashioned roses, lavender, honeysuckle and philadelphus assail the nostrils to remind us that there are more ways of appreciating plants than by sight alone. The days and nights are milder; pots, tubs and hanging baskets may be safely left outside and the gardeners at Brockhole are busy planting out half-hardy annuals, bedding plants and vegetable seedlings.

There are a large number of school groups using the grounds, learning about the National Park and the local environment through planned activities and trails. Their favourite spot however is always the Adventure Playground, where they can let off steam between lessons.

Working with children...

Can you remember what it was that first sparked your interest in gardening? It might have been a visit to someone else's garden, or a specialist nursery, a TV programme, or the acquisition of a garden with a new house. For many of us, I suspect our interest began when we were introduced to the subject as children, perhaps encouraged to have a small plot of our own or shown how to sow seeds at school.

Nowadays, with schools having to concentrate on SATS results and the three Rs, there seems to be less and less time for extra-curricular activities such as gardening. At home, children are surrounded by high-tech entertainment and gardening with parents or grandparents has to compete with computers, TV, Playstations and so on. So any gardening they can be enticed into doing should be carefully chosen to capture their interest and imagination, perhaps introducing them to a low-tech but extremely satisfying hobby that may last them a lifetime!

At Dalemain, near Ullswater, a children's garden has been planted where all the plants have common names that include

Rosa 'Bobbie James'

animals, such as catmint, dog's-tooth violets, and squirreltail grass. This is a lovely way of introducing children to plants, but for hands-on gardening it is hard to beat fruit and vegetables. Most children enjoy sowing seeds and can be encouraged to grow runner beans, courgettes, pumpkins and salad vegetables. The prospect of being able to eat the results can be very encouraging, and some kids may even be persuaded to eat vegetables that they would normally refuse, if they have grown them themselves!

Since my husband is reluctant to give over any precious planting space to vegetables, Michael and I have been making use of grow-bags on one of the paved parts of our garden. Each year our back yard proudly sports six tomato plants, bought at the school fete, and planted by my son and his friends. The tasks of regular watering and feeding, pinching out side shoots and tying in the plants as they grow can be all be done by the boys, and the end result will be some tasty fruits that they can help themselves to with pride!

Children are also fond of growing flowers, though their choice of what looks good varies wildly from grown-up tastes! In my experience they prefer larger and brighter flowers than their parents, and would rather grow sunflowers, nasturtiums, snapdragons and chrysanthemums rather than anything more subtle. They like things that grow tall, and things that climb, such as sweet peas and climbing beans. They also like plants that they can grow indoors, preferably in their own rooms; spider plants, amaryllis lilies, cacti and succulents for example.

All children should be taught the difference between edible and ornamental plants. They should know never to put any plant into their mouths unless they are sure that it is safe to eat. There are so many toxic and poisonous plants in our gardens that it would be impossible to label them all. And anyway, not all children can read!

... and animals

Being a bit of a dog lover, I was interested to read an article in a dog magazine about making a pet-friendly garden. As the owners of a boisterous three-year-old bull terrier, we have been rather more concerned with making our garden 'dog proof' rather than 'dog friendly', but the magazine article had some good tips for making the garden and the dog less mutually exclusive.

Firstly, a dog owner's garden needs to contain the said animal securely and safely. Stout boundary fences and gates are a necessity, but with the ranges of ornamental fencing available today these need not be an eyesore. Areas where young children play, or where your most precious plants are growing, could be separated from the doggy bits with lighter decorative fencing or trelliswork. Many dogs like a sunny spot on warm paving on which to sunbathe, they should also have a patch of shade to retreat to when they get too hot! It's not too difficult (even with a bull terrier) to teach your pup to relieve himself in a particular area of the garden. If this is an area of paving or gravel then it can easily be washed down and disinfected at regular intervals. Dog urine can burn grass, so an area of lawn is not recommended.

The article suggests that delicate or precious plants be put into containers for protection against trampling. I would also suggest that your pots and planters be filled with loam or John Innes compost, as these are heavier and more difficult for a dog to turn over (I speak from bitter experience here!). Another good tip was to use pliable, multi-stemmed plants such as grasses, willows and bamboos, rather than those with single stems or brittle branches. These are less liable to be broken off, and if they are damaged they are quicker to grow back. To deter canine short cuts it suggested using dense planting, with stout, prickly shrubs such as berberis or holly, at points where the dog is most likely to want to break through. At home, we have surrounded our main flowerbed with a low box hedge, it looks attractive and only the appearance of next door's cat will tempt the dog to vault over it.

As with children, it is important not to grow any plants that might be poisonous or irritating to your pet. Avoid the obvious things like *Aconitum* (monkshood), laburnum and foxgloves; most good suppliers are now labelling toxic plants. Weed killers can also be dangerous to pets, always read the instructions and exclude animals and children from the treated areas for the recommended times after spraying. Other garden products that can be dangerous to dogs include slug pellets and cocoa shells, again look out for warnings on the product labels.

Foxgloves

My first recollections of foxgloves are of those surrounding the foxy whiskered gentleman in the 'Tale of Jemima Puddleduck', and I have had a soft spot for them since I was a child. Their rich purple colour, the bold spotting inside the trumpet-shaped flowers and their attractiveness to industrious bumble bees are their principal assets in my view, together with the fact that they will grow and seed themselves almost anywhere with very little input from the gardener. I agree that they can be invasive, but it is a simple matter to cut off the old flower heads to prevent seeding, or to weed out young seedlings before they get too big.

Foxgloves are at home either in the herbaceous border or naturalised in woodland, but it should be remembered that all parts of the plant are poisonous and so they are best avoided where there are small children about. Our native foxglove, *Digitalis purpurea*, is quite variable in colour, ranging from deep purple, through pink, to white. Cultivated varieties are now available for those looking for something less commonplace. The 'Excelsior Hybrids' have large flowers arranged evenly all round the stems, in pastel shades of creamy-yellow, pink and purple, whilst 'Sutton's Apricot' has, as its name suggests, apricot pink flowers.

Altogether there are 22 other species of foxgloves, natives of countries like Spain, Italy, the Balkans, Lebanon and north-west Africa. Not all are easy to obtain as plants but most will grow easily from seed, which is more readily available. Remember that many foxgloves are biennials or at best short-lived perennials, so when they flower it is important to collect and sow some of the seed in order to keep the plant in your garden. *Digitalis grandiflora*, the yellow foxglove, has large, pale yellow flowers with brown stripes inside, whilst *Digitalis x mertonensis*, a hybrid between our native foxglove and the yellow foxglove, has short spikes of flowers the colour of crushed strawberries.

Another common woodland native, Solomon's seal, also has exotic relatives that are worth growing in the garden. Whorled Solomon's seal, *Polygonatum verticillatum* flowers each June at Brockhole; it has the same familiar, green and white hanging flowers as its cousin, but the foliage is much thinner and more delicate, carefully and evenly whorled around the stems. In a good year spherical red fruits are supposed to follow the flowers, but I have yet to see them on our plant.

Texture in the garden

When adding a new plant to a border, most of us will spend some time thinking about the colour of the flowers and foliage of the existing plants, and how they will match with those of the new-comer. We will also think about the relative heights of the plants, so as not to place tall things in front of shorter plants. We may even go so far as to think about the balance between flowers and leaves, the amount of bright flower colour weighed against the softer greens and greys of foliage.

Leaves can be used to add another aspect to the design of beds and borders; which is texture. The dictionary definition of texture is "the feel or appearance of a surface or substance"; it is the soft, misty appearance of fennel, the furry feel of lambs-ears and the spiky, prickly look of New Zealand flax, red-hot poker and iris leaves. Just as a garden without colour can look dull and uninteresting, a garden without a range of textures will look flat and two-dimensional.

Kniphofia

Large, flat leaves such as those of *Hosta*, *Gunnera*, *Angelica* and *Rheum*, the ornamental rhubarb, will contrast well with smaller flowers and foliage; soft and woolly leaves such as those of *Verbascum* and *Phlomis* will add a different texture again. Any species or variety of fern will add a soft and lush effect; the royal fern, *Osmunda regalis*, is great for the back of a bed, reaching up to 6 feet in height. The more leathery foliage of the hart's tongue fern has a shiny, slightly crinkly look to the fronds. Similarly the leaves of most species of grass will add a spiky texture, whilst the feathery flower spikes have quite a different effect. Taller grasses include the well-known pampas grass, *Cortaderia selloana* and golden oats, *Stipa gigantea*. Grasses for smaller gardens might include the blue fescue, *Festuca glauca*, and the squirreltail grass, *Hordeum jubatum*.

It is not only leaves that add texture to the garden, many flowers such as oriental poppies, sea hollies, astilbes and *Gypsophila* have unusual textures. Background plantings such as hedges and lawns add yet more differing textures to the canvas that is your garden! In fact, once you start thinking about it, it is not only plants that add texture to the garden. We should also consider the effect of paths, walls, fences, and trellises for example. Would that path look better with the small scale, rough warmth of brick paving, or does it need the cooler, smoother effect of paving slabs?And what about that jumper you were thinking of wearing to mow the lawn in, would it be better in cable-knit or mohair . . . ?

Parthenocissus

Edwardian photographs of Brockhole show the walls of the house covered in some kind of climbing plant, and in order to recreate this style enjoyed by the original owners, we have allowed a couple of plants of Virginia creeper (*Parthenocissus quinquefolia*) to romp over the front of the building. They have put on masses of growth, reaching right up to the roof; the green, five pointed leaves turning a stunningly rich crimson each autumn, looking (in some lights) almost as if the walls were on fire. Now however, due to the imminent arrival of painters, the gardeners have had to take down this huge expanse of foliage, cutting right back to two or three main stems, only a few feet from the ground. I approached this task with some trepidation, feeling sure that the creeper would have damaged the masonry and woodwork whilst on its mission to cover every available space!

Parthenocissus, a relative of the grapevine, in the family Vitaceae, climbs using tendrils. Each tendril is tipped with sucker-like pads that attach themselves to supports such as walls and fences. Much to my surprise, the stems pulled away from the masonry quite easily, leaving behind most of the tendrils, which were subsequently brushed off with a wire brush. The rendering was unharmed, and may indeed have been protected from the weather by its leafy covering. Not all was sunshine and roses however! Several patches were completely out of the reach of our ladders, and where branches had grown behind an obstacle such as a drainpipe or gutter their expansion was beginning to put considerable strain on the pipes and fixings. Around some of the window frames the extra dampness had undoubtedly encouraged some rotting of the wood.

So the moral of this story is; whilst it is safe to allow Virginia creeper to grow over the walls of your house, keep it clipped back from window frames, do not let it grow behind gutters or downpipes, and *never* let it get beyond the reach of your secateurs!

There are several other species of *Parthenocissus* available; one of the prettiest is *P. tricuspidata* 'Lowii', which has deeply cut and crinkled leaves. *P.*

tricuspidata, the Boston ivy, is similar to Virginia creeper except that its leaves are divided into three instead of five. The cultivar *P. tricuspidata* 'Veitchii' has leaves with wavy margins that turn a deep purple rather than crimson each autumn. *Parthenocissus henryana* is a species I am not familiar with, but it is supposed to have velvety green or bronze leaves with white or pinkish veins. One to look out for....

Dogwoods

The gentle pastime of garden visiting is an excellent way of

spending summer weekends, looking at other people's gardens has always been a good way of picking up new ideas and of discovering new plants. Often there is the opportunity to buy plants and other souvenirs, there is the possibility of meeting and talking to other gardeners, and there is even the chance that your own garden may look better in comparison and so boost your horticultural confidence.

Last June, I went with a gardening friend to a garden open day at Gresgarth Hall, near Caton. The gardens were looking lovely, with the added attraction of plenty of interesting garden ornaments and mosaic paths to amuse the children. A group of plants that particularly caught my eye was a fine collection of *Cornus*, the flowering dogwoods. Dogwoods come in many shapes and sizes of shrubs and small trees. Some, such as *Cornus alba* and its cultivars, are grown mainly for their colourful winter twigs. Others, such as *C. alternifolia*, the pagoda tree, are grown for the elegance of their branches, the delicacy of their foliage and their bright autumn colour. Those that are flowering now are prized for their showy bracts; four large, white or pink, petal-like structures that surround the insignificant flowers. At Brockhole we grow *Cornus kousa* var. *chinensis* and *Cornus kousa* 'China Girl', their greeny white bracts that gradually turn pink before fading always attract a great deal of attention from visitors.

One dogwood that caught my attention at Gresgarth Hall was *Cornus* 'Norman Hadden'. It is a small tree that may eventually reach 25 feet tall and almost as far in spread, with creamy white bracts up to 4 inches across produced in early summer. It was growing amongst a group of shrubs and the bracts stood out in an almost luminous way against the various greens of the background foliage. Flowering dogwoods also come in pink; *Cornus florida* and its cultivars 'Cherokee Chief' and 'Spring Song' have rose pink bracts. The bracts of many of these dogwoods are followed in autumn by strawberry-like, fleshy red fruit (not edible unfortunately) and many of them give a fine show of autumn colour.

One more flowering dogwood to mention; a shrub that is so short that its common name is creeping dogwood. It is *Cornus canadensis*, a native not only of Canada but of northern USA, Greenland and northern Asia as well. It reaches only 6 inches in height but it has the same showy bracts as its taller cousins, about 1 inch across and framed by a whorl of bright green leaves. I have had a specimen of *C. canadensis* for many years but it refuses to spread and is little bigger now than when I planted it; in the right position it can form great carpets of ground cover, especially in woodland or shrub borders.

Irises for damp gardens

I have long been jealous of those people with warm, sunny gardens and well-drained soils, who can grow bearded irises in their borders. I love the delicate but elegant blooms of these irises together with the range and mix of colours on their petals. Sadly for me they do not like the damp soils at Brockhole and refuse to flourish here as I would like. All is not lost however. Their cousins the Siberian irises are ideal for damper soils; unlike the bearded irises whose surface rhizomes like to bake in the sun each summer, these irises prefer a moist, humus rich soil and are not deterred from flowering by a bit of Cumbrian rain! Originally from central Europe, Turkey and Russia, *Iris sibirica* has fine, grass-like leaves up to 18 inches tall, forming generous clumps that can be easily divided every few years to make new plants. Even without the flowers this foliage adds an interesting texture to the beds in which it grows.

The blue-violet flowers are produced in early summer, four or five to a stem, held well above the leaves. There are two types of petals in irises, the 'falls' or pendulous outer petals and the 'standards' or inner, upright petals. In *Iris sibirica* both falls and standards are veined with a deeper blue, and the blue of the falls changes to white near the centre of the flower.

The plant breeders are rapidly realising the potential of these tough, yet beautiful plants, and there are now many different varieties of Siberian irises to choose from. We have been growing 'White Swirl', a creamy white variety tinged with yellow at the centre, and 'Cool Spring', a pale blue variety, for several years now. Both have made bold and attractive plants and are a

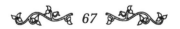

valuable addition to the garden in early summer. More recently, I have planted 'Dreaming Yellow' which has fine, creamy white standards and slightly ruffled, yellow falls, and 'Tropic Night' which I am not quite so fond of – the blue is of a very purple hue and contrasts oddly with the yellow and white veining.

For those with very wet gardens who long to grow irises, the solution can only be *Iris pseudacorus*, our native flag iris. Quite happy to grow in any kind of damp or even downright wet spot, the bright yellow flowers of flag irises can be seen in the wild flowering in all kinds of boggy places at this time of year. There are several different shades of yellow to be had, together with a white variety, *I. pseudacorus* 'Alba', and a variety with variegated leaves, *I. pseudacorus* 'Variegata'.

Jobs for June

❀ Now that overnight frost is unlikely it is safe to plant out half-hardy annuals and perennials, and to put out hanging baskets for the summer.

❀ Collect seed from spring flowering perennials such as primulas, erythroniums, violets and hellebores as the seedpods ripen. Many will germinate best if sown while still fresh.

❀ Stake taller perennials such as delphiniums, before the wind knocks them over.

❀ Trim back winter flowering heathers this month, cutting back last year's growth but not cutting into the old wood.

❀ Prune shrubs such as weigelia that flowered in May and early June. Clematis montana can be cut back now if it is getting out of hand.

❀ Take care when pruning shrubs and climbers not to disturb nesting birds. Better to wait until any nestlings have left before continuing.

❀ Clip back aubretias, arabis and perennial candytufts when they have finished flowering.

❀ Having planted out the summer bedding it's time to think about next winter and spring! Sow hardy annuals such as wallflowers, forget-me-nots and Brompton stocks in trays or on a spare patch of ground, for planting out in the autumn.

❀ Keep greenhouses and conservatories well-ventilated, water in the cool of the evening or early morning to ensure a thorough soaking and to avoid leaf scorch.

❀ Keep an eye out for vine weevil damage, both inside the greenhouse and outside. Water infected plants with the biological control, Nemasys H.

July

At this time of year, on fine sunny days, we are often blessed with the comment "I wish I had your job" from visitors and office staff. The short reply "come back in November and you can have it!" sums up the gardeners' viewpoint – we need the memory of these good days to see us through the cold, wet months of winter.

This is the month when much of the planning and planting of previous months (and years) comes to fruition – sometimes quite literally. Suddenly the herbaceous perennials are in full bloom, the bedding plants and half-hardy perennials fill their allotted spaces, hanging baskets and pots seem to expand and overflow with colour. In the kitchen garden the soft fruit is ripening, apples are swelling, and the vegetable plot begins to look as if it might produce a generous crop. No time for the gardeners to relax; July can be quite a rainy month, the weeds and grass continue to grow quickly and it's often a battle to keep the garden looking trim between the showers.

Chilean plants

There must be a part of Chile that has a climate and soils similar to our own in Cumbria. There are several excellent trees and shrubs from that country that grow well in our gardens, enjoying the mild, wet summers and also the mild wet winters!

Probably the best known of this select group, though none of them are as well known as they ought to be, is the monkey puzzle tree, *Araucaria araucana*. It is a large conifer, reaching 50 to 80 feet high in cultivation, with characteristic leathery leaves, arranged spirally on the branches and sharp enough to deter most monkeys I should think! The *Araucaria* was first introduced to England by Archibald Menzies in 1795. It is said that he pocketed some nuts put out for dessert whilst dining with the Governor of Chile. He sowed the nuts whilst on board ship, and landed back in England with five small plants ready to be planted out at Kew..

I have written about the Chilean firebush, *Embothrium coccineum*, several times but its brilliant orange flowers are so striking that it is surely worth another mention. It was introduced to our gardens in 1846, when it was collected by William Lobb for the nursery of Messrs Veitch. The plant hunter Harold Comber later collected hardier forms from higher altitudes and it is these that do best in our gardens today. Another Chilean far from home is the Chilean lantern tree, *Crinodendron hookerianum*. This plant was also collected for Veitch by William Lobb and it must have caused quite a stir when it was introduced to the public in 1848. It is an evergreen shrub, or small tree, with stiff pointed leaves of dark, glossy green. In early summer, the branches are covered with rich crimson flowers, hanging beneath the foliage like bells or lanterns. Curiously the flower stalks are produced in autumn, but do not open until the following year. Both these shrubs prefer an acid soil and a sheltered position away from cold winds.

The Chilean holly, *Desfontainea spinosa*, spends much of the year cunningly disguised as an ordinary Holly bush. Then in July it reveals itself in its true colours, producing masses of red and yellow tubular flowers that last well into the autumn. Surprise, surprise, it was collected by Lobb in 1843, and again by Comber in 1925. Like the previous two shrubs it prefers a sheltered spot with a non-alkaline soil.

Wildflower meadows

At this time of year the countryside of Cumbria is dotted with fields full of wildflowers and grasses waiting to be mown for hay. They look lovely from the roadside and a closer look reveals the number and variety of different species that join to make up the whole rich patchwork. For the last 14 years at Brockhole, we have devoted our largest field to the growth of wildflowers. With careful management, or healthy neglect whichever you prefer, we have increased the number of wildflowers and grasses to over 100 different species. In May, June and July, with paths mown

through it for easy access, it is a fascinating place to wander and look at the flowers together with the associated insects and birds.

There are two main aspects to managing a wildflower area. The first is to keep the soil fertility as low as possible, because fertilising will encourage the growth of coarse grasses that will quickly smother the more delicate species. So this is where the healthy neglect comes in; no fertiliser or manures need to be added at any time of the year. The second aspect is the cutting regime; the area must be mown around about the beginning of August and the hay raked off (taking a crop of hay also helps to lower the fertility of the soil.) The grass is then kept at a low height until growth begins in the following spring. At Brockhole we graze a flock of sheep on the meadow during the winter months, they keep the grass wonderfully neat and their hoofs break up the turf allowing seeds to reach the soil and germinate. For the last few years we have borrowed a selection of rare-breed sheep from Jennie Hill at Greenholme in Penrith, and our meadow has been clipped by Shetland, North Ronaldsay and Soay sheep amongst others. They seem to be tougher and less inclined to roam than modern breeds, and they are certainly an interesting topic of conversation for winter visitors to the gardens.

It is now relatively easy to buy seed to sow your own wildflower meadow. The key is to prepare the soil carefully, making sure any perennial weeds such as docks and dandelions are dug out, before sowing your wildflower seed mixture. It is possible to buy different mixtures depending on soil type and aspect; most contain a blend of grasses, annual wildflowers and longer lasting perennial wildflowers. Once your area is established you can add to it by planting in new wildflowers (buy these from a nursery, *never* dig up plants from the wild.) If you have got the conditions right, Mother Nature will be tempted to join in, and new species will turn up by themselves from time to time, brought as seeds by the birds, by the wind or in trouser turn-ups!

Butterflies in the garden

With the disappearance of so many wildlife habitats from our countryside, Britain's gardens are becoming increasingly important as safe havens for wildlife. Butterflies in particular miss the variety of plants that have disappeared from our fields and hedgerows, and will come into the garden looking for nectar for themselves and food for their caterpillars. The number and variety of butterflies in a garden will obviously depend on site and location, but we can make our gardens more attractive to butterflies, and encourage them to visit, by planting nectar-rich flowers and by leaving food plants for caterpillars in strategic spots.

Almost everyone knows that the common name for *Buddleia* is the butterfly bush, and many of us will know of butterflies' preference for the autumn flowering ice plant, *Sedum spectabile.* But there are many more shrubs and herbaceous plants that they will feed on. At Brockhole I have particularly noticed them feeding on lavender flowers and catmint. They adore hebes and the bedding plants alyssum, aubretia, French and African marigolds. In the herb border, butterflies will visit thyme, marjoram, sage and bergamot, and elsewhere in the garden they feed on phlox, michaelmas daisies, sweet rocket and red valerian. In autumn, I have seen scores of red admiral butterflies feeding on windfall apples, and in the spring there are often small orange-tip butterflies around cruciferous plants such as lady's smock and arabis. Honeysuckle is another favourite, as are the insignificant looking flowers of ivy.

Food sources for caterpillars are unfortunately less attractive to the gardener, but if an odd corner or bank can be left for them the reward will be more butterflies to grace the rest of the garden. If you are lucky enough to live near open countryside, the fields and hedgerows around about should be able to supply food for the caterpillars of the peacock butterfly. Those of the red admiral feed mainly on nettles, while the caterpillars of the painted lady prefer thistles. Tortoiseshell caterpillars feed on the leaves of willow, elm and other trees. Other less common species feed on plantains, docks, knapweeds and grasses.

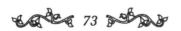 *73*

Perhaps this is just the excuse we have been looking for not to weed that overgrown part of the garden!

Microclimates

We are all quite familiar with the overall Cumbrian climate. Mild, wet winters without the long periods of frost or very cold weather suffered by other parts of the country, and damp, warm summers with never quite enough sunshine! Then too, every garden in Cumbria has its own particular climate, depending on such factors as height above sea level, distance from the coast and exposure to prevailing winds. Within these local climates, each garden contains its own microclimates. Areas that are south facing are the warmest spots in a garden, east- and west-facing areas catch the morning and afternoon sun respectively. Walls are great heat trappers, absorbing the sun's warmth during the day and slowly radiating it back out during the night. The soil beneath hedges can be dry and poor, that beneath large trees is dry, poor and shady; beds at the top of slopes tends to be freer draining than those at the foot of slopes, and so on.

The cleverest gardeners are those who exploit these microclimates fully. They know every inch of their gardens, from the warmest, most sheltered parts to the wettest and windiest corners. Armed with a knowledge of the conditions each plant prefers, they are able to match the plant to the position, sure in the knowledge that it will perform to the best of its ability. The rest of us must arrive at the same conclusions by trial and error! If a shrub has turned yellow when grown in full sun, we dig it up and try it in a more shady part of the garden. We can split plants and try them in several different sites to check which they like best. We plant things in pots and move them around to see where they are happiest, (remembering that pots have their own microclimate – they dry out quickly in warm weather, the soil will rapidly become impoverished if not fed regularly, and in winter they may freeze solid.)

The worst mistakes lead to the loss of the plant, the greatest successes lead to spectacular results. The large passion flower growing round our back door in Cockermouth (less than 35 miles from the Scottish border) is one such success, another is a huge clump of arum lilies that grows in the small bed in our yard. Both are frost-tender, but flourish because of the extra warmth and shelter provided by the house and garden walls.

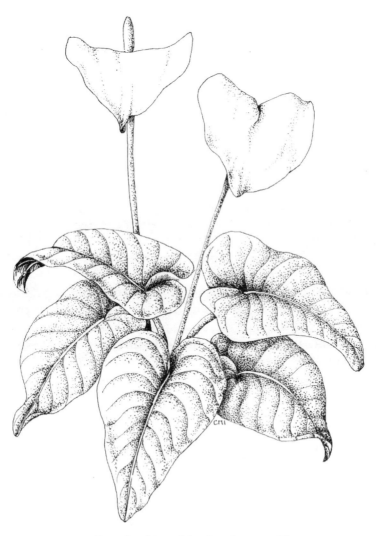

Zantedeschia aethioptica, the arum lily

Bog gardening

At my son's junior school, some of the parents have built and planted a bog garden. Each bed is constructed as you would a garden pond – dug out to the shape and depth required, lined first with damp sand and then with a plastic or butyl liner, the edges of the liner held down with turf or paving. But instead of filling the liner with water, they have filled it back in with soil so that it will become a fine place for growing plants that require a high level of moisture. If it gets too wet, all they need to do is puncture a few holes in the liner with a garden fork.

Now, many of us living in the Lake District have beds and borders which have a high level of moisture without a butyl liner and without the luxury of the garden fork remedy! This need not be a problem however, and it is more satisfying I think (and cheaper) to plant bog plants rather than go for more costly options such as drainage schemes and soil improvements.

Some of my favourite moisture loving plants are ferns and there are generally quite a few to choose from in garden centres and nurseries these days. *Osmunda regalis*, the royal fern, is one of the largest, growing up to 6 feet tall and having elegant, bright green fronds. The fertile fronds, the fern equivalent of flowers, are tassel-like, rusty brown and held above the plant at the end of taller fronds. The ostrich fern or shuttlecock fern, *Matteucia struthiopteris*, is smaller and more delicate, with fronds arranged in the shape of a shuttlecock. This fern spreads by underground rhizomes and, in a few years, will build up to form an attractive group. For those with lime-rich or alkaline soils, the hart's tongue fern, *Asplenium scolopendrium*, is an elegant, evergreen with rich green, leathery, tongue-shaped leaves. (Why do most ferns have such unwieldy Latin names?)

If you prefer something brighter for your bog garden, you need look no further than the primulas. The candelabra primulas, which, as the common name suggests, have tiers of flowers on tall stately stems, come in a variety of colours including pink, red, yellow and orange. They are quite easy to grow from seed and look particularly good planted in drifts either in a single colour or in a tapestry of mixed shades. If you have plenty of space, and like to make an impression, then *Gunnera manicata* is the ideal architectural plant. A perennial, with each leaf up to five feet across, the whole plant can be more than seven feet high. At the other end of the scale, its cousin *Gunnera magellanica* has leaves only an inch or so across. They are rounded and glossy, reddish when young and rich, deep green later on, borne on creeping stems which will form a mat of foliage given time. The perfect bog plant for a miniature bog garden?

Astilbes, hostas, *Iris sibirica*, bergenias, foxgloves, hellebores, skunk cabbage, arum lilies, ligularia, globe flowers, willows, dogwoods... the list of plants which positively prefer a moist or wet soil is rich and various. So next time it's too wet to mow the lawn, or raining when you should be weeding the flower beds, spare a thought for our drought-plagued southern counterparts and think of all the wonderful plants which we can grow so easily in our rainy climate.

Hi-tech bird boxes

Although we work in an Edwardian garden, often using traditional styles and organic methods of cultivation, the Brockhole gardeners are always keen to embrace new technology if we think it will benefit the gardens. To this end, we have taken delivery of some new, state-of-the-art bird and bat boxes. They are called 'Schwegler' boxes, made from a mixture of concrete and wood, using only natural materials and additives in their construction.

The first thing you notice on picking up one of these boxes is the weight – they are surprisingly heavy compared to a wooden box. The makers claim that the density of the 'woodcrete' allows a much more stable environment within the box, with temperatures heating up and cooling down more slowly than in a traditional box, a sort of birdy air conditioning! Another advantage of this material is that it can be used to make a large range of different shapes, I assume it can be made in moulds of almost any design. Thus there are not only the usual bird boxes for blue tits, flycatchers and nuthatches, there are also specially shaped ones

for swallows, swifts, housemartins and a whole range of other birds. The main disadvantage is that they are all more expensive than normal boxes, but having said that they are designed to be in operation long after a wooden box would have rotted and collapsed.

The bat boxes look very similar to the bird boxes, except that they have a small entrance slit at the base, rather than a round hole at the top. Unlike wooden boxes that need slats inside for the bats to hold on to whilst roosting, the woodcrete is rough enough for them to hold on to directly. Bats will use these for their summer roosts; there are much thicker, winter hibernation boxes available, which weigh a staggering 28 kg – quite a feat to haul up into a tree or roof space!

We will be trying out three bird boxes, which will join our traditional wooden ones in trees in the grounds, together with a pair of housemartin nests that will go under the house eaves, and two swallow boxes that will be placed inside one of the balcony alcoves. We have also bought three summer-roost bat boxes that we will be putting in trees along the lakeshore at Brockhole. Bats are often to be seen here on warm summer evenings after sunset, feasting on the multitude of small insects that fly above the surface of the lake.

Climbing and rambling roses

Having talked a great deal in the past about the virtues of old-fashioned and shrub roses, I'm now going to start on climbing and rambling roses! What nicer way to appreciate the shape, colour and scent of rose flowers than when they are at head height or looking down at you from above. They can be used to decorate house walls, to cover trellis, pergolas and obelisks, to climb through shrubs and trees, and to cover shabby sheds and outbuildings. Climbers will flower all summer whilst ramblers will put on a shorter but no less spectacular aerial display.

Rambling roses generally have large numbers of smallish flowers, in bunches or sprays held on robust stems. The smallest ramblers are between 10 and 15 feet tall, the largest can be over 30 feet. They send up strong new growths from the base of the plant each year, these can be tied in to a framework or left to scramble where they please. There is no need for much pruning, just take a few of the oldest stems back to ground level after flowering. We have several rambling roses growing at Brockhole, including 'Albertine' and 'Alberic Barbier' that grow along the wall at the back of one of the herbaceous borders. 'Alexander Girault' is growing over an old tree stump outside the offices, 'Paul's Himalayan Musk' is scrambling through an apple tree, and 'Bobbie James' is covering the arch at the entrance to the rose garden. I love them all for their tough, careless attitude to life, not to mention the fact that they seem to thrive on minimal attention from the gardeners.

Climbing roses are a different matter. They are too often simply tall versions of hybrid tea and floribunda roses and although their flowers are bigger and the flowering season is longer than for ramblers, they need more attention. The stems are shorter and more branched, they need tying in at regular intervals, with stems trained horizontally to encourage the formation of flowers, cutting side shoots back to the framework of main stems in spring. They can be more prone to diseases such as blackspot and mildew and may need routine treatment with fungicide to look their best. Heights vary from 8 to around 15 feet depending on the variety. At Brockhole our best climbing rose is 'Meg' which flowers all summer on the kitchen garden trellis, our worst is 'Zephirine Drouhin', near the Orangery, which has usually lost most of its leaves from blackspot by mid summer.

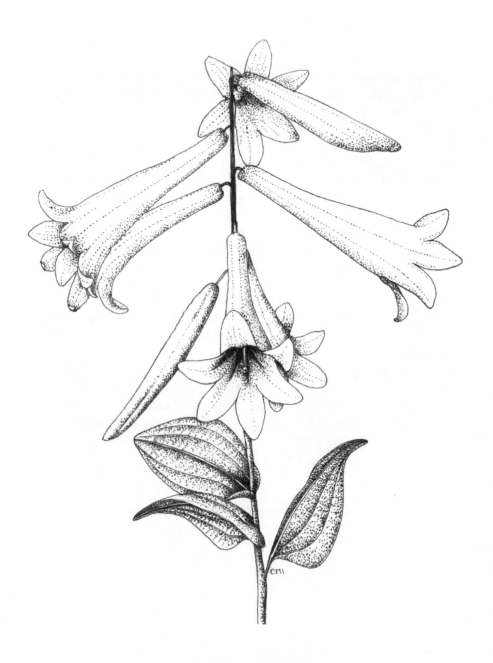

Cardiocrinum giganteum

Jobs for July

❀ Summer prune apple and pear trees. Cut back all long growths to three or four buds from the main framework; this will let in light to ripen the fruit, and encourage the formation of next year's fruit buds.

❀ Clean out and disinfect the greenhouse whilst it is relatively empty. Repairs and painting can be done on rainy days.

❀ Take cuttings from hardy shrubs and alpines such as olearias, helianthemums and penstemons.

❀ Gather herbs for winter use before they begin to flower. Tie them in small bunches and hang them to dry in a cool airy room. Alternatively, try freezing fresh herbs in ice cubes.

❀ Deadhead herbaceous perennials and roses to encourage new flowers and to extend the flowering period by preventing seed heads from forming.

❀ Mow lawns weekly to keep them in trim, but if the weather turns dry raise the height of cut to prevent browning and scorching of the grass.

❀ Clear around the base of trees and shrubs planted in grass, leaving a generous circle free of weeds around the base. This will reduce competition for light, water and nutrients.

❀ Continue to feed pot-grown lilies after flowering has finished, to build up the bulbs for next year.

❀ Feed tubs, pots and hanging baskets weekly, taking off any spent flowers to keep them looking fresh.

❀ Summer prune wall-grown Japanese quince (*Chaenomeles japonica*) and pyracantha, cutting back side shoots to two or three buds from the main framework.

August

High summer! Not often a dry and sunny month in the Lakes, August is much more likely to be a succession of humid, rainy days, glowering skies interspersed with blasts of brilliant sunshine that light up the lake and fells.

It is an odd time for the garden, a constant battle to keep things flowering that only want to go to seed. Soft, summer growth on trees and shrubs is bent over by heavy rain; we have to patrol the garden regularly, trimming back soggy branches overhanging paths and seats. On fine days, many visitors spend their time by the lakeshore, wandering up through the terraces in search of cool drinks and ice creams from the café.

The wildflower meadow is cut this month (it's the right time now that everything has finished flowering). The whole field will be needed for the Bank Holiday events programme.

Plant conservation

August and September are the months when we clip the yew hedges and topiary at Brockhole. For several years we have collected the clippings and, along with other gardens all over the country, sent them to a pharmaceutical company that turns them into a drug called Taxol (the Latin name for yew is Taxus). Taxol is used in the treatment of breast cancer, and it was nice to think that our humble clippings were being of use in the world of medicine. More recently, the pharmaceutical industry has developed synthetic Taxol, and our clippings are not such hot property, but the whole process left me wondering about other plants in our gardens. How many more of them might be hidden cures for diseases and viruses, just waiting to be discovered by science? It's not just tropical rainforests that hold the key to the medicines of the future, our humble English gardens may be just as important!

Another garden plant that regularly turns up in pharmaceutical products these days is the evening primrose, the oils being widely used in homeopathic medicine. In addition, several

The pergola at Brockhole

species of evening primrose (*Oenothera*) make excellent garden plants, with spikes of large, deep yellow flowers produced throughout the summer months. *Oenothera biennis* is, as its name suggests, a biennial, whilst *Oenothera fruticosa* is a perennial; both flower not just in the evenings, but throughout the day.

As fashions in the horticultural world come and go, so plants are introduced to and lost from our gardens on a regular basis. Many old varieties of flowers, fruits and vegetables are now lost forever, remembered only in people's memories and in old nursery and seed catalogues. The National Council for the Protection of Plants and Gardens (NCCPG) is a body set up to stem this tide of losses and to help save endangered garden plants. It runs a National Collections Scheme, where individuals, nurseries, parks and larger gardens are encouraged to adopt a species or genera, and to collect and grow as many varieties of those plants as possible. There are now over 600 collections, all open to the public (some by appointment only) ranging from abelia and acacia through to yucca and zelkova. All are listed in the NCCPG directory, which is published each year; the whole scheme is like a huge, living reference collection for the use of gardeners and scientists alike.

Whilst we are on the subject of conservation, how many people are still using peat-based compost? Gardeners account for 70% of all the peat used in this country, of which 60% comes from the UK. Peat is a non-renewable resource, and the peat bogs from which it comes are the home of many rare plants, reptiles, insects and birds. These peat bogs cannot be replaced or replanted, and the plants and animals that live there cannot be rehomed. This is not habitat destruction in the Amazon or Indonesia, which we can do little about, this is wildlife conservation on our own doorstep, where we gardeners can have a powerful impact! There are plenty of substitutes now available, so we should make a concerted effort *not* to use peat in our gardens.

Hedge clipping

Back to hedges ... we have several hundred metres of beech and yew hedges to clip at Brockhole, together with some topiary yew balls and two large holly hedges. By August the beech and yew have made up most of this year's growth, and the birds have generally finished nesting in them. If we had trimmed them earlier, not only would we have disturbed any nesting birds, but the hedges would have carried on growing afterwards and would probably have needed a second clipping by the autumn. All our hedges are cut to an 'A' shape, with the bottom of the hedge wider than the top. This ensures that light reaches all the leaves, and the bottom branches stay as thick and leafy as the top. 'A'-shaped hedges are somehow more aesthetically pleasing than straight-sided hedges, and definitely more horticulturally pleasing than 'V'-shaped hedges, which are generally gappy at the base and look as if they might fall over at any moment.

The beech hedges are cut using a petrol-driven hedge trimmer; although noisy and quite heavy, it is fast, manoeuvrable and efficient. In complete contrast, the yew topiary is cut using hand shears. These give the finest cut of all and are easier to manage when climbing frequently up and down the ladder to check on the shape of the bush. The yew hedges, close to the main house, are trimmed using an electric hedge trimmer. This is much quicker than using hand shears, but gives a finer cut than the petrol-driven machine (which tends to leave little stalks of bare wood protruding from the top of the hedge.) It's also less noisy for our visitors.

Summer shrub pruning

After 'V'-shaped hedges, my pet gardening hate is shrubs that have been pruned with shears or hedge trimmers, to look like leafy lollipops. The correct way to prune flowering shrubs is to wait patiently until they have finished flowering. As a rough guide, the best time to prune any shrub is after the last blossoms have faded. The exceptions are those that flower in autumn, these are best left alone until early spring. The next job is to remove any dead, dying or misshapen branches, cutting them out right at the base of the plant.

Now we come to the nitty gritty! Do not, ever, be tempted to get out the shears and give your plants a number-two haircut. Not only will they look ridiculous, you will in all likelihood be removing a large proportion of next year's flower buds. Get down low and examine the stems of the shrub. Look for the oldest wood, usually a darker colour and with tougher bark than the newest stems. Then cut most of these old branches out at the base of the plant, aiming to remove about one third of the whole shrub. The younger stems that remain will flower next year, and you will have let enough light and air into the centre to encourage more new shoots to grow. Repeat this process every year, removing stems on a three-year cycle, and you should always have vigorous flowering material and a respectably shaped bush to boot!

For all pruning, make sure you use a sharp pair of secateurs. For larger cuts I use a pair of loppers or better still a small pruning saw, trying to avoid making ragged cuts which are slower to heal and may allow disease to enter.

Anemones and geraniums

The hardy geraniums or cranesbills are an important and invaluable mainstay of many gardens throughout the summer months. Not to be confused with greenhouse or bedding geraniums (more correctly known as pelargoniums), they have soft foliage, colourful flowers and the ability to flower for long periods of time. My gardening encyclopaedia states that there are around 300 different species of hardy geraniums, though some of these are annuals. Most however are perennials, they will come up year after

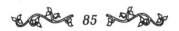

year, requiring the minimum of attention from the gardener, apart from a little shearing every now and then to remove spent flowers and older leaves (these are herbaceous plants not shrubs so shearing is allowed!).

One of the most popular species is *Geranium macrorrhizum*, a spreading plant with semi-evergreen, strongly aromatic leaves. There are several varieties, with flower colours ranging from white to purple. It grows as happily in shade as in full sun, I like to plant it close to paths so that the scent is released as people brush past. A smaller, more compact plant altogether, *Geranium x cantabrigiense* also comes in several shades of white, pink and mauve. The evergreen leaves are a glossy mid-green and the whole plant spreads slowly by runners to form a dense groundcover mat. Smaller still is *Geranium dalmaticum*, one of my favourite perennials and almost compact enough to be called an alpine or rock garden plant. It grows well in shallow tubs or along the top of walls, producing bright pink flowers throughout the summer months

Geranium endressii 'Claridge Druce' is a popular choice of pale pink geranium, though its habit of seeding itself around can make it a bit of a nuisance if you are not looking for robust ground cover! Better to plant *Geranium* 'Wargrave Pink' which is a similar colour but less generous with its progeny. For unusual foliage it is hard to beat *Geranium renardii*, a plant originally from the Caucasus. Its leaves are slightly wrinkled, velvety and grey-green in colour, the flowers are pale lavender, boldly veined with deep violet. For spring flowering choose *Geranium phaeum*, the dusky cranesbill, and its cultivars; for blue flowers choose *G. wallichianum* 'Buxton's variety' or *G.* 'Johnson's Blue'. For the brightest flowers of all choose *Geranium psilostemon*; a native of Turkey this plant has the most brilliant magenta flowers, guaranteed to brighten up the dullest corner of the garden.

Most hardy geraniums are easy to grow, requiring nothing special in the way of soil type or cultivation. They are easily propagated by dividing the clumps in spring, or by sowing seed in containers out of doors in the autumn.

Two particularly valuable perennials that come into flower this month are the Japanese anemones, *Anemone hupehensis* and *Anemone x hybrida* or *Anemone japonica*. There are dozens of different varieties of these tough, reliable herbaceous plants, in many shades of white and pink. They flower through late summer to mid-autumn, with elegant saucer-shaped flowers held gracefully above generous clumps of leaves that vary from bright green to dark purple in colour. When other plants begin to show signs of flagging or going to seed in late summer, or when bad weather knocks more delicate flowers about, the Japanese anemones can always be relied upon to give a great show.

Purple foliage

In the last few years it has been fashionable to grow plants with grey and silver foliage, and no garden should be seen without its full compliment of artemisias, helichrysums, lavender and sil-ver-leaved helianthemums. Sadly for those of us who live in Cumbria, our high rainfall means that many of these trendy plants (whose leaves are adapted to cope with hot, dry weather) don't do very well in our Lakeland gardens. I've lost count of the number of lavenders we have had to replant due to losses from wet weather, and in retaliation I think we should be at the fore-front of a new trend – for growing plants with purple foliage!

There are dozens of plants with purple foliage, ranging from trees to alpines. They look great as background planting, their dark leaves a foil for brighter plants; they also look well in a mixed border, the purple tones mixing surprisingly well with bright colours such as reds, yellows and even oranges (in a hot sort of way!) Together with pinks and whites, purple foliage plants look extremely classy, and as specimen trees and shrubs set in grass they are hard to beat.

Here is a selection of my favourites; beginning with the purple elder, *Sambucus nigra* 'Guincho Purple'. This is a robust shrub, reaching 6 to 10 feet in height, the foliage is a rich, deep purple and the flowers, produced in early summer, are a delicate froth of pale pink fading to dark rose. *Cotinus coggygria* is a shrub of similar size with rounded or oval leaves of deep reddish purple; in late summer masses of tiny flower stalks form smoke-like plumes above the foliage, giving it its common name of smoke-bush. The variety 'Royal Purple' has the deepest foliage, whilst 'Notcutt's Variety' has darker pink plumes.

The purple berberis *B. thunbergii f. atropurpurea*, with its

Kitchen garden sundial and lavender hedge

brilliant show of autumn colour, and *Photinia* 'Red Robin' with its showy red new growths, are valuable small shrubs that will fit in most gardens. The herbaceous perennials *Heuchera* 'Palace Purple' and the purple-leaved form of the common yellow loosestrife, *Lysimachia punctata*, are reliable border plants, and for border edges the purple form of the common celandine, *Ranunculus* 'Brazen Hussey' is a real eye-catcher. There are purple-leaved bedding plants, such as the dahlia 'Bishop of Llandaff', and purple grasses like *Melica altissima* 'Atropurpurea'. There are even purple-leaved climbers, for example *Vitis vinifera* 'Purpurea' the purple grapevine, and a purple-leaved ivy, *Hedera helix* 'Atropurpurea'.

Food for thought

Most gardeners know of the importance of feeding hanging baskets, pots and tubs; the plants in them grow fast and furiously, using up available nutrients almost as quickly as they are added to the compost. Plants in a container or basket that hasn't been fed look thin, with yellow leaves and small flowers that quickly run to seed. They are not fussy as to the source of their nutrients, it can be slow-release granules, watered on soluble fertiliser or a foliage spray of liquid feed. As long as there is plenty of it they will be happy. Again, most gardeners are well aware of the need to add fertilisers to soil that is growing vegetable and fruit crops, to replace the goodness removed as the crop is harvested. This is often in the form of compost, manure or other bulky organic matter, whilst a more immediate boost can be given by feeding a top dressing of poultry pellets or watering with a liquid feed.

We are not quite so good at remembering to feed the more permanent plants in our gardens, such as trees, shrubs and hedges. As guilty of this as anyone, I was intrigued to read of a new type of 'bio-organic' fertiliser, originally produced for lawns but now being used with great success on roses and other shrubs. We duly acquired a sackful of this new fertiliser and applied generous amounts to the old-fashioned roses at Brockhole in early spring. The fertiliser is supposed to add beneficial bacteria and fungi to the soil that help to unlock nutrients, bound up in the soil and previously unavailable to the plants, as well as improving soil structure and water availability. Now it may just have been that the weather was kinder than usual, or that we pruned more carefully or at just the right time, but after using this fertiliser, the roses were really good – full of flower and hardly any blackspot or mildew to be seen. So we applied the rest of the sack to some azaleas, a newly planted hedge, a couple of sickly trees and a number of other shrubs that look as if they could do with a boost. I await the results with interest.

One group of plants that I am reluctant to feed is the herbaceous perennials. I like to keep the soil around them in good heart, through the occasional addition of organic matter (usually applied as a mulch that the worms can break down) but additional feeding produces tall, soft growths, that are inclined to flop and fall over after rain or windy weather. A shorter, tougher perennial will flower just as well but will require little or no staking – good news for the busy gardener!

Holiday time

Besides the obvious pleasures of being away from work, of soaking up a good deal of much needed sunshine and of the opportunity to improve my snorkelling technique, one of the main pleasures of a holiday abroad for me is the chance to look at for-

eign plants. On a holiday in northern Greece, where temperatures are a little cooler and damper than on the Greek Islands, we
were too late to see many native wildflowers, which tend to be
spring flowering. In the mountains, the woodlands are similar to
our own, with stands of beech, oak, sweet chestnut and pine. We
were pleased to spot groups of *Cotinus coggygria* (smoke bush)
and *Arbutus* (strawberry tree.) On lower ground there were tanta-
lising glimpses of seed heads, and we promised ourselves a return visit one Spring.

What grabbed my horticultural attention then, were two other
groups of plants; crops growing in the fields and smallholdings,
and plants growing in gardens. I love to see fields of olive trees,
nectarines, sweetcorn, tobacco, tomatoes, grapevines, kiwi fruit,
aubergines and courgettes all growing robustly outside whilst
we have to grow them in sheltered conditions in this country.
The scent from orchards of ripening peaches will last in my
memory for a long time, and the family joke about every street
corner having a watermelon seller will probably last almost as
long!

Although the gardens of northern Greece receive a steady
summer baking, there were several heavy showers of rain whilst
we were there, and there seems to be no shortage of water for
irrigation purposes. Many houses and apartments were bordered
by green lawns, the grass a little coarser than ours and copiously
watered by hose each evening. The walls and balconies were
generously draped with vines and flamboyant climbers such as
Bougainvillea and *Campsis*, with the scent of white jasmine and
honeysuckle filling the air each evening. Most gardens sported at
least one lemon tree, and *Hibiscus* and *Nerium oleander* were
also very common. Some Australian plants such as *Callistemon*
(the bottlebrush) and *Eucalyptus* seemed to have found a
home-from-home there, as had some fine specimens of banana,
date palm and *Agave*. Other familiar garden plants included
petunias, French marigolds, *Cistus*, roses, dahlias and salvias.

Top of my list of favourites however was the humble red
geranium (*Pelargonium*) which was planted in window boxes,
tubs and gardens all over the region. Its bright colour against the
white and cream walls of the houses, echoing the terracotta red
of the tiled roofs, seemed for me to be the epitome of a Mediterranean summer.

Jobs for August

❀ Cut beech and yew hedges this month.

❀ Take advantage of fine, dry weather to treat wooden benches, fences and trellises with wood preservative (remember to use a plant-friendly brand.)

❀ Take cuttings of bedding and greenhouse geraniums (pelargoniums).

❀ Cut long grass that has been grown for wildflowers. Allow any ripened seeds time to drop off before raking up the cut grass.

❀ Collect seeds from annuals such as nasturtiums, love-in-a-mist, calendulas and nicotiana. Store them in paper envelopes in a cool, dry place until next spring.

❀ Prune back the canes of summer-fruiting raspberries to ground level once they have finished cropping

❀ Clip back lavender bushes lightly to remove the old flower heads.

❀ Take cuttings of hydrangeas; they root best if inserted singly in small pots, minimising root disturbance when they are potted on.

❀ Take time out to wander around the garden and make a note of any gaps to be filled or plants to be moved. It can be difficult to remember where they were once they've finished flowering or died down for the winter.

❀ If you are going away on holiday, arrange for a friend or neighbour to water pots and hanging baskets. If you are not going away, volunteer to care for a friend's garden while they are away — a change is as good as a rest!

September

*I always feel a sense of relief when September arrives.
The children go back to school and our visitor numbers become
suddenly fewer, reduced from hundreds of possible critics to a
select number of true garden visitors who will appreciate the
garden and plants for what they are and not just for their
pretty effect.
The first cold nights and the first tints of autumn colour
arrive almost simultaneously, and we begin to turn our
attention from routine maintenance to planning the jobs that
will take up our time during the winter months.*

Seed heads

Coming back from a holiday it is always interesting to see how the garden has changed in the couple of weeks that we have been away. Some plants have grown and come into flower, others have begun fruiting, and the lawn has always grown twice as fast as it does when we are at home! But no matter how short the holiday, and no matter how caring the friend or relative you leave in charge of watering and feeding, there is no real substitute for the TLC that you can provide on a continuous basis. In our back yard, carefully tended by my sister in our absence, the slugs have had a field day and the leaves of the runner beans have turned yellow through lack of feed. You can't expect garden sitters to deadhead the bedding and basket plants either, and these are rapidly going to seed and ceasing to flower. The remedy is to go over them carefully and pinch out every faded flower or seed head; they will look a little bare at first, but will soon pick up and should continue flowering for another few weeks or so.

Once September has arrived though, I feel it is quite acceptable to have some plants in the garden sporting seed heads instead of flowers. Indeed with some plants the seed heads are almost as pretty as the flowers, and can be used to prolong the 'flowering' season. Others are not quite so decorative, but will

Hanging basket by our front door in Cockermouth

provide important food for birds and small mammals through autumn and early winter. The seed heads of annuals such as love-in-a-mist and scabious 'Paper Moon' are obvious examples, as are those of teasels, clematis and the ornamental grasses.

Others are less obvious, but once you get into the habit of thinking before you cut off faded flower heads there are plenty more. Some species of *Rodgersia* have strong spikes of golden brown seeds, and many of the umbellifers, including the tall herb angelica, hold their seeds in smart poses. Many herbaceous geraniums have long, pointy seed pods that split along their lengths as the glossy black seeds ripen; the rounded capsules of poppies are especially ornamental and can be cut and dried for indoor flower arrangements. The seed heads of the giant Himalayan lily, *Cardiocrinum giganteum,* are up to three inches long, pale brown, with toothed edges almost like small creatures.

Only one word of caution – these ornamental seed heads are generally full of seeds, and the plant's aim is to spread as many seeds as widely as possible throughout the garden. So make sure any seed heads you do leave are not those of invasive weeds or of vigorous plants that will be difficult to weed out next summer!

Late summer colour

The end of summer can be a difficult time in the garden; most shrubs have long finished flowering, many herbaceous plants are going to seed and even the bedding is beginning to look rather battered. There are, however, several groups of plants that are still looking good, bravely bridging the gap between summer and autumn. In our biggest mixed border at Brockhole, the phlox are putting on a fine show, and although the individual flowers are not always perfect, the overall effect is good. Behind the phlox there are shrub roses that flowered in early summer. Many of these are now sporting bright orange and red ornamental rose hips; my favourites are the chocolate brown hips of *Rosa glauca* that contrast so well with the purplish grey of the foliage.

In amongst the phlox the foliage and seed heads of the euphorbias are providing some useful colour, as are the papery seed heads of astrantia. Other late-flowering herbaceous plants include pink and white Japanese anemones, deep blue *Agapanthus* or African lilies, penstemons, purple *Geranium procurrens*, and the stately grey foliage of the Scotch thistle, *Onopordum acanthinum*. This last one is a biennial that has slowly begun to seed itself into the borders at Brockhole. In its first year, it makes a robust rosette of spiny grey foliage; in its second year it throws up a flower spike of architectural proportions, often up to 6 feet tall, crowned with purplish pink, thistle-like flower heads.

At the front of the border are several useful ground cover plants, such as *Polygonum runcinatum* from the Himalayas, *Ajuga reptans* in several different forms, variegated, green and purple, hostas (now badly eaten by slugs and slightly scorched by a hot spell), *Ourisia* 'Loch Ewe' and acaenas. Where there are gaps in the cover we have planted a few annuals and half-hardy perennials; the most effective being several varieties of *Cosmea*, their upright feathery foliage has stood up well and the shapely pale pink or white flowers have lasted for a long time.

Gardeners' day out

Every year, the Brockhole Gardeners have an annual outing, to a garden show or to one or two gardens further afield than our Cumbrian neighbours. It gives us a chance to see what the opposition is doing, to see new plants and plant combinations, to pick up fresh ideas and simply to have a day out together, away from the confines of work! On one such occasion, we visited Ryton Organic Gardens at Coventry, headquarters of the Henry Doubleday Research Association, and a Mecca for all aspiring organic gardeners. I generally reckon to spend two to three hours going round an average-sized garden open to the public; if I tell you that we spent nearly seven hours at Ryton it will give you an idea of how interesting it was!

I say interesting rather than attractive, because it is not particularly pretty in a conventional way. At first glance, it even looks a little untidy. But the 20-acre site has so many different techniques and ideas to see and learn about that after a while this hardly matters. The site is divided into a number of smaller demonstration plots and gardens, including a herb garden, an allotment, an ornamental kitchen garden, rose gardens, a bee garden, soft fruit and top fruit plots and a special needs garden. In all there are over 30 different plots, all managed entirely by organic methods. There is even a reed bed sewage treatment system!

One of the things that I was most interested to check out was the level of pests and diseases. All pathogens are controlled without the use of chemicals, and I was prepared to be very critical and to label as unacceptable any signs of damage or sickness. The trouble was that I couldn't find any – everything looked remarkably healthy! This is achieved through strict crop rotation, by using companion plants to attract beneficial insects, by planting resistant varieties, and by using biological control, barriers and traps. In addition, they were keeping the soil as healthy as possible through cultivation techniques and the judicious addition of organic material. Weeds are also kept in check without the use of chemicals, using different types of mulch and green manures, and planting closely to leave no room for invading weeds.

For children there was a play area, some fascinating woven willow structures, a human sundial and the biggest flower pot in the world – seven feet tall and weighing one and a half tonnes! The Ryton shop sells loads of goodies for organic gardeners including a wide range of books, and the café has excellent home-grown food. What more can I say – a great success all round.

Sculpture in the garden

Aside from pots and urns, the use of sculpture in a garden is always controversial. From marble to stainless steel, ceramic to lead, traditional to modern, Capability Brown to Henry Moore, most styles have their proponents and their ardent critics. I'm not qualified or inclined to pass judgement on sculpture in general, but I will say that a well-chosen and sited piece can light up and compliment an area of planting in a way that a simple container or piece of furniture can never do.

At Brockhole we have acquired not one but thirteen pieces of artwork, loaned to us by Cumbria Arts in Education and sited throughout the grounds and garden margins. They are part of the Skylines project, where two poets and two artists worked with Cumbrian schoolchildren in fourteen different schools, to produce these innovative sculptures. Each one represents a different area and aspect of Cumbrian life. The stone or metal used reflects the materials local to each school, and the words carved into each piece were written by the schoolchildren 'in response to their immediate landscape'. Some are limestone, some slate, some red sandstone, others are metal, incorporating glass or mirrors. The one from Barrow looks uncannily like a nuclear submarine! All of them have poetry, carved in expressive lettering or precise calligraphy, on their sides or faces.

Because the gardens are Edwardian, listed by English Heritage, and traditional in style, we have not placed any of the artwork within the formal terraces. Rather we have put them at the edges and in the grounds where most have blended in remarkably quickly with the shrubs and meadow surrounding them. After six months, some have almost disappeared, though others still look a little out of place. So what do I think of them? Some of them I like very much, others I am not so sure about! I find the poetry much more difficult than the sculptures themselves, the textures and shapes are easier to deal with than

Holly hedge border and statue

the words. But I do like the ideas behind Skylines, and I love the sculptures as a whole project, as an area for discussion and debate, and as a modern contribution to an established site. The only way to see what I am blathering on about is to view them for yourselves. A leaflet showing where they all are is available from the information desk at Brockhole.

Hydrangeas

As leaves begin to change colour with the onset of cooler days and nights, there are precious few shrubs still flowering in the garden as autumn approaches. One group of shrubs that continues to decorate the borders well into the season is the hydrangeas, tough, sturdy shrubs with a wide variety of different shapes, sizes and colours. The most common of the hydrangeas grown in gardens is *Hydrangea macrophylla*. Originally from Japan, there are now many cultivated varieties that can be divided into two groups, the lacecaps and the hortensias. In both cases the colour of the flowers depends on the amount of aluminium in the soil; acid soils tend to produce blue and purple flowers whilst alkaline and neutral soils favour pink and red. On neutral soils, the flower colour can be changed from pink to blue by the addition of a blueing compound. White flowers are not affected by soil type.

The lacecaps have large flattened flower-heads, with a centre of tiny fertile flowers surrounded by a halo of larger, more showy, sterile flowers. In contrast, the hortensias have spherical heads, consisting entirely of sterile flowers, giving rise to their other common name, the mop-head hydrangea. Of the lacecaps, my favourite is a low-growing variety called 'Blue Wave', the sterile flowers are a rich blue-purple at Brockhole with the fertile flowers a deeper contrasting shade of blue. Of the hortensias, I prefer a variety called 'Preziosa', which grows to a height of 4 to 5 feet. At Brockhole its flowers are a rich mix of red, pink and bronze-purple, quite difficult to describe but wonderful to look at! The colours change gradually as the flowers age, and like many hydrangeas they are good candidates for drying.

Other species of hydrangea that can be seen in gardens include *H. aspera* from eastern Asia, *H. quercifolia* from the south-east of the USA, *H. paniculata* from Russia, China and Japan, and *H. serrata* from Korea and Japan. All are of the lacecap style, the first three making bushes up to 10 feet high. They are excellent additions to large shrub borders, where their grand ornamental flowers provide valuable colour in late summer. *H. serrata* is much smaller, forming a compact bush around 4 feet in height and spread. The variety 'Bluebird' is a rich blue as its name suggests, whilst the variety 'Grayswood' has mauve fertile flowers with sterile flowers that start white and gradually fade to dark red.

Seaside gardening

My family and I spent a long weekend one September staying at my sister's house in Whitley Bay, on the north-east coast, trying unsuccessfully to escape the Cumbrian rain! Thinking it might be useful for Cumbrian gardeners with seaside homes, and also for those with exposed, windy sites inland, I set myself to walk the streets, making notes of those few (so I thought) plants that can survive the battering of bitterly cold north-easterly winds.

I was expecting the usual 'toughies' that gardening guides advise for planting in such conditions, and these were certainly present – hedges of *Griselinia littoralis* and *Escallonia*, hydrangeas and montbretias, shasta daisies and *Lysimachia*. But I was quite unprepared for the variety of other plants, not just surviving but flourishing under these rough conditions. The shrubs included the Japanese quince (*Chaenomeles japonica*) *Elaeagnus*, various hebes, purple-leaved *Berberis thunbergii atropurpurea*, variegated hollies, fuchsias, *Ceanothus*, potentillas, the smoke bush *Cotinus coggygria*, buddleias, cotoneaster and even a reasonably sized rhododendron! Trees were obviously finding the going quite tough; many were stunted and some were definitely sickly. However beech trees were growing quite well, as were the rowans (*Sorbus intermedia* and *S. aucuparia*) some cherries, sycamore and sumach. Conifers find the combination of salt and wind almost impossible, the only Leylandii hedge I found was badly burned. Scots and Corsican pines will grow in exposed conditions, often sculpted by the wind into bizarre leaning shapes.

It was the variety of herbaceous plants that most impressed and surprised me. I saw impressive clumps of *Bergenia* and *Alchemilla* (ladies mantle), subtle combinations of catmint, *Dicentra* and Japanese anemones, drifts of *Helleborus corsicus*, euphorbias, fennel and asters, and elegant pots full of lilies and hostas (without slugs!) There were masses of annuals and biennials brightening up front gardens all along the street, and walls and trellises were covered with honeysuckle, *Clematis montana* and *C. tangutica*, and several ornamental varieties of ivy.

My sister has decided not to fight the harsh climate but to 'go with the flow' and plant things that are native to coastal regions. After visiting several local nurseries and plant sales she has amassed a small collection of perennial grasses: *Festuca glauca*, *Stipa gigantea*, *Pennisetum villosum* and *Miscanthus sinensis* 'Gracillimus' a greeny-yellow grass with narrow leaves that turn a rich bronze in late summer. With these, she has planted groups of sea pinks (*Armeria maritima*) the deep, rich blue of *Agapanthus*, a purple-leaved New Zealand flax (*Phormium tenax*) and two different species of the sea-holly, *Eryngium bourgatii* and *E. alpinum*. These last produce round, thistle-like heads of metallic blue, surrounded by blue bracts and soft spines, which are excellent for dried flower arrangements. The whole area is mulched with two to three inches of pea shingle, together with some groups of larger beach-sized cobbles, which will conserve moisture and save on weeding. The garden edges are made of large pieces of driftwood which my sister and her family have found whilst beachcombing.

Ferns

When the weather is wet, the ground is too soggy to walk on and the unfinished gardening jobs begin to pile up, I take comfort in the fact that all this water means damp conditions that are ideal for growing ferns. There are over 40 species of fern native to Cumbria and several of these can be found decorating our gardens and walls, uninvited but nevertheless welcome guests.

The commonest is *Polypodium vulgare*, the common polypody, a bright evergreen fern with stiff, narrow, divided fronds and coppery coloured, creeping rhizomes – when it finds a spot that it likes, preferably a wall or rock garden, it will cover the area with a ferny carpet of green. Another native that loves walls, clinging to the smallest of cracks, is the maidenhair spleenwort, *Asplenium trichomanes.* This is a semi-evergreen fern, with delicate slender fronds around six inches long, supported by glossy black midribs. It prefers limestone soils, which may explain why it is so often found on walls, growing on the lime in the mortar.

A close relative, but much more choosy about whose walls it graces, is the rusty-back fern, *Ceterach officinarum* – similar in size and shape to the spleenwort, but the backs of young fronds are covered with a soft, silvery 'rust' which matures to a reddish brown as the frond ages. A fern which we struggle to grow in the acid soils at Brockhole but which thrives on the alkaline soils around Kendal is the hart's tongue fern, *Phyllitis scolopendrium.*

As its common name suggests, the leaves are tongue-shaped, leathery and a glorious bright green throughout the year. At Brockhole it grows only in cracks in the paving and often underneath top-water drain covers, where it can have alkaline conditions, shade and plenty of moisture, rather like artificial limestone pavement!

Naturalised in the Lake District, and definitely appreciating our moist climate, is *Onoclea sensibilis*, the sensitive fern. I bought a small specimen from a plant sale at Sizergh Castle many years ago and we now have a large clump of this handsome fern decorating a corner of the garden. It's a tough, creeping plant, with deciduous, arching fronds that turn a lovely yellowish-brown in autumn. It has no special preferences and needs no special attention (other then plenty of moisture) seeming to thrive on neglect – a fact that endears it to me enormously! Last, but not least (even though it is one of the smallest ferns), I should mention *Gymnocarpium dryopteris*, the oak fern. This is a delightful, delicate little fern, with frothy, rich green fronds that tilt at right angles to the light. It is another spreading plant, but this one will only move a few inches each year; preferring a humus rich soil, it is ideal for moist, shady spots.

Please remember that while it is fine to split bits off ferns in friends' gardens (with their permission of course!) it is illegal to collect them from the wild.

Jobs for September

❀ Prune rambling and climbing roses, cutting out any dead or diseased wood, tying in new growths and removing some of the older stems to ground level. Tying stems in horizontally will encourage the production of flowering side shoots for next year.

❀ Cut back catmint and hardy geraniums lightly after they have finished flowering, they will often reward you with a second flowering in autumn.

❀ Sow grass seed between September and mid October, so that it has the chance to germinate and establish before winter.

❀ Scratch up the surface of any bare patches in the lawn, using a garden fork or rake. Sprinkle with grass seed, which will germinate quickly and cover the gaps.

❀ Raise the height of mower blades and cut less frequently as the cooler weather slows down growth.

❀ Prune hydrangeas after the flowers have gone over. Lightly remove the old flower heads, then cut around one third of the oldest stems down to ground level to encourage new growth.

❀ Keep an eye on the weather forecast. Low temperatures may mean turning on the heat in the greenhouse, while frost warnings will mean protecting dahlias and other tender bulbs and corms.

❀ Plant daffodil bulbs in rough grass. When planting them in borders, mark where they are so you don't dig them up again later!

❀ Many hardy, evergreen herbs will root readily from cuttings taken this month. Select shoots six to eight inches long, cut close beneath a joint, and place in a free-draining compost or a compost/sand mix. Experiment with rosemary, lavender, sage and thyme.

❀ Order spring bulbs for planting outdoors, and for growing in bowls indoors. Use a specialist bulb firm such as de Jaeger or Parkers Dutch Bulbs, the choice is much wider than in the shops and the prices more reasonable.

October

This is an in-between month in the garden – most of the basic maintenance work, such as mowing, edging and weeding, slows right down, yet it seems too soon to start on winter tasks and projects. For most of the month, the Centre is quiet, with few visitors and only one or two school parties each day. When half term comes, the place is suddenly busy again. Families with small children and dogs visit the playground and lakeshore, the shop and information are decorated with Halloween spiders and bats, events leaders are drafted in to paint children's faces, and to make willow spiders' webs and witches brooms with them.

Garden seating

For some people gardening is an everyday chore, with mowing and weeding to be fitted in between the hoovering and ironing. For others, time spent in the garden is precious, leisure time snatched from a busy schedule, to be used as efficiently as possible before going back to the everyday chores of life. How many of either group have time to sit in the garden and do nothing but enjoy the view and the flowers?

Not many I guess, which probably accounts for the lack of seating in most gardens. A well placed garden seat or bench can be so much more than somewhere to rest your tired muscles at the end of a stint of gardening. It can be part of the framework of the garden, drawing the eye to a particular area, or setting off a group of plants that might have been overlooked if left to their own devices. It can be a focal point at the end of a border, leading you down towards it, or it can be part of a formal arrangement of clipped hedges and topiary, almost like a piece of sculpture or a garden ornament.

When choosing sites for seats or benches, it is important to consider where the sun shines at different times of the day. I like to have seats in both the morning and evening sun, with seats in

Kitchen garden seat

the shade for the middle of the day. Then it is imperative to have a bench close to the kitchen door, so that even if you are caught up in household chores you can stop and have your tea break outside. A seat at the end of the garden looking back towards the house is often an unusual way to view the garden, and seats in out of the way corners can be useful for a little peace and quiet away from the rest of the family! There are many different types and styles of seating available, ranging from wood to stone to iron, and from single seats to benches to hammocks. Colour is an important consideration; white plastic chairs can be very difficult to site, (difficult even to look at in bright sunlight!) but wood, in its natural state or painted with a muted woodstain, will fit into most gardens. Homemade benches, constructed from logs or planks can fit in really well, but make sure they are steady and safe to sit on!

Finally, having chosen your seats and benches and placed them in strategic places around the garden, it is well worth investing in some easily portable seats, such as canvas "directors" chairs. That way when unexpected guests turn up, your cosy seat for two on the terrace can be quickly converted into a friendly setting for morning coffee or evening drinks, without anyone having to sit on the kitchen stool!

Witch hazel – *Hamamelis mollis*

Coloured winter stems of dogwoods

Decorative seed heads

Phygelius 'Yellow Trumpet'   *Rudbeckia fulgida* 'Goldsturm'

Ranunculus ficaria – 'Brazen Hussy'

The phlox border in August

Crinodendron hookerianum –
Chilean lantern tree

Embothrium coccineum –
Chilean firebush

Cercidiphyllum japonicum and
Betula utilis

Onopordum acanthium –
Scotch thistle

Phormium tenax – New Zealand flax

Pots in the backyard, including
Narcissus 'Thalia'

Helleborus orientalis

Memorial trees

A little while ago, we had a special visitor to Brockhole – Mr. Thomas Mawson, grandson of the Thomas H. Mawson who designed and built the gardens here at the turn of the last century. We had a fascinating talk about his grandfather, and about the work he did at Brockhole and elsewhere. As we walked around the garden we were surrounded by trees and shrubs that were planted by the elder Thomas around 100 years ago. What a legacy to be able to leave one's grandchildren, and what a wonderful way to be able to remember one's grandfather.

In the fourteen years that I have worked at Brockhole we have planted many tens of trees that will come to maturity in several decades time, just as Mawson's trees have today. Some have been woodland and lakeshore plantings, native trees such as oak, ash, alder and Scots pine. Others have been specimen trees for the gardens and grounds, such as tulip trees, a handkerchief tree, cedars and *Nothofagus*. Some of the trees we have planted have been extra special; they are memorial trees planted to commemorate particular events. We have planted trees as memorials to loved ones who have passed away, as reminders of distinguished visitors or particular dates, and (my favourites) we have planted trees to commemorate the births of children. My own son, Michael, has a lime tree, planted for him by his godparents after his christening at the age of 6 months. He comes to visit it regularly, I hope that he will still be able to visit it when he is an old man and it is a stately, mature specimen 80 to 100 feet tall.

We have planted several trees to mark the arrival of the new millennium. In particular I have planted some sweet chestnut seedlings, grown from seed collected a few years ago, from a tree in the grounds that may have been planted by Thomas H. Mawson 100 years ago. I wonder if a future head gardener will be collecting seeds from my trees in another 100 years time? Not everyone is as fortunate as I am in having lots of space and opportunity to plant for the future, by imagine if we all managed to plant just one tree each to mark the new millennium. How much greener and more pleasant would be the lives of future generations of Cumbrian gardeners!

 *105*

Garden compost

There is much satisfaction to be had in making garden compost. It has a great deal to do with the recycling aspect; being able to turn grotty, garden-waste products (such as used bedding and annual weeds) into a rich soil additive, with no cost other than a bit of elbow grease. But it's partly the magic of the process itself; that grotty garden waste *can* be turned into crumbly, brown organic matter, with help only from the gardener and a bunch of worms and soil organisms!

Over the years, through trial and error, it has gradually dawned on me that what making compost is really all about is mixing and turning. Firstly the mixing. Adding a variety of different wastes (grass clippings, weeds, kitchen waste, autumn leaves) in small pieces is the secret of good compost. Tougher, fibrous materials maintain structure in the heap, leaving space for air to circulate, whilst soft, sappy materials break down more quickly and provide easy food for microbes to work on. Most things organic can be composted as long as they are mixed in the right proportions. The Brockhole gardeners are currently experimenting with compost made from a mixture of grass clippings and shredded paper. Our first attempts were rather slimy, so we have had to increase the amount of paper, and incorporate small amounts of wood chippings in order to let more air into the mix. The results are quite promising.

Then the turning. Compost needs to be turned regularly to allow air to enter and activate the microbes in the heap, raising the temperature sufficiently to destroy weed seeds and other nasties. The more often a heap is turned or mixed up, the quicker the plant material will break down. There are some short cuts that can help in the pursuit of perfect compost. Worms are great for helping with the turning; when starting a new heap I like to add a bit of old compost, or a barrowload of old horse manure, containing a good number of worms to help the new heap get started. Compost accelerator, usually ammonia or urea, helps to heat up a compost heap, speeding up the decomposition process. Grass clippings in small amounts are good for this too. A tarpaulin or waterproof lid can prevent the heap from becoming too wet and cold, whilst a good watering in dry weather will keep the process rumbling on.

Containers for compost are easily made and can be as simple as a post and wire construction lined with old carpet or cardboard, as long as it is covered to keep the rain out and the warmth in. Two or three bins in a row are excellent as the compost can be turned from one into the next and a second heap can be started whilst the first rots down. There are plenty of different types of bins for sale in DIY stores and garden centres; choose one that fits your garden and which is appropriate for the amounts of waste you will have. If you intend to compost kitchen waste it's a good idea to have a sturdy, solid bin to discourage unwanted visitors to the heap; on the other hand an old drainage pipe tucked down the inside of a compost heap can provide a cosy winter home for hedgehogs.

Buying plants

Where do you buy your plants? The local garden centre? A nearby nursery? School fetes? Gardens you visit whilst on holiday? By mail order from specialist nurseries? These are all good sources of plants, especially for impulse buys; you didn't know you needed that plant until you saw it, but now it is a must for your garden! Friends too can be an excellent source of plants, seeds and cuttings; there are few folk so generous as keen gardeners when it comes to sharing plants. But what if you are looking for a specific plant? You may have seen it on TV, or in a gardening book or magazine. It may have looked just right for that empty space in the garden or you may be thinking of building up a collection of a particular group of plants. You may have seen a specimen growing in some other collection where you don't know the gardener, and where plants are not for sale. What do you do then, if your normal sources do not stock this exact plant?

Fear not, for help is at hand at your nearest library or bookshop! Every year the Royal Horticultural Society produces an amazing paperback called 'The Plant Finder.' Subtitled '70,000 plants & where to buy them', this book is a lifesaver for anyone who has set their heart on a special plant and wants to know where to find it. Firstly plants are listed alphabetically, by genus, from *Abelia* to *Zizyphus*, and then each entry has a list of species and cultivars in cultivation. This in itself is a revelation; did you know, for example, that there are over 700 varieties of hosta? (including one called 'Elvis Lives'!) Then, each species or cultivar has a list of nurseries that sell it, with symbols denoting new entries, synonyms, awards of merit, variegation and so on. If there is a national collection of a particular group this is also marked.

At the back of 'The Plant Finder' is a section devoted to nurseries. This section is divided into regions, and nurseries within each region are listed alphabetically by name. For each nursery there is an exact address, telephone and fax numbers, contact names, opening times, mail order and catalogue details, together with the type of plants that they specialise in. There are even regional maps to pinpoint each nursery, an invaluable aid for the planthunter on holiday! All in all a remarkable book, deserving a place in the library of every keen plantsperson.

Golden plants

In the section for August I wrote of my fondness for plants with purple and bronze foliage. At this time of year, when the nights begin to close in and the days can be dull and dreary, I am partial to plants with yellow or golden foliage. In the summer months their glowing colours can be overshadowed by brighter flowering specimens, but during autumn golden foliage really comes into its own, particularly if combined with the reds and purples of autumn leaves.

The golden elder, *Sambucus racemosa* 'Plumosa Aurea' makes a fine shrub for a gloomy corner of the garden. Its delicately cut foliage is bronze when young, maturing to golden yellow, there are typical creamy-yellow elder flowers in spring and occasionally red fruits in autumn. It can reach a height of up to 10 feet but is easily pruned to keep it smaller if needed. For lower-growing ground cover, and for stem colour through the winter, the almost luminous yellow foliage of *Cornus alba*

Golden Hop

'Aurea' is a good choice, especially for a shady area. To keep the stems bright and the foliage fresh it is important to cut the growth back almost to ground level each spring, so that new stems are regularly produced.

Recently, we planted some specimens of *Berberis thunbergii* 'Aurea' at Brockhole. They took a long time to establish but, once they had settled, their foliage was literally brilliant; they bear small, golden-yellow leaves on compact, bushy plants, together with spines and red autumn berries in true berberis fashion. For various reasons we have moved then to a new spot and they are no longer looking quite so happy; they obviously do not like their roots to be disturbed! One yellow foliage plant that is very popular at present is the golden Mexican orange-blossom, *Choisya ternata* 'Sundance'. This small, rounded evergreen shrub has glossy, bright yellow leaves that have a noticeable scent, there are fragrant white flowers produced in late spring and often again in autumn. For reasons I am unable to justify, I am not a big fan of this plant, but I have seen one growing in a large pot and I have to admit it looked superb! It may be slightly tender, so it would be best planted against a wall or in the shelter of larger trees or shrubs.

Other good golden foliage plants include *Caryopteris clandonensis* 'Worcester Gold', *Lamium maculatum* 'Aureum', the golden hop *Humulus lupulus* 'Aureus', Bowles' golden sedge *Carex elata* 'Aurea' and the golden-leaved thymes, ivies and hostas.

New hedges

I was thinking recently about the materials that we use nowadays to mark the boundaries of our gardens. It is quite usual to see new fences, brick and stone walls being put up in local gardens, but I can't remember when I last saw anyone planting a new hedge. Hedges are much cheaper to plant than the cost of bricks or fencing, but they do require a little patience whilst they establish. This may be the reason for the decline in newly planted hedges, since we have been encouraged by the media to plan for instant effect.

Hedges have several distinct advantages over walls and fences. Firstly they make excellent windbreaks. Faced with a solid structure, the wind tends to rise up and then eddy over the barrier, creating rough currents at the base, precisely the effect one is trying to prevent. With a hedge, the force of the wind is broken up as it passes through the plants, so that only a mild breeze reaches the other side. Secondly, hedges make good barriers to noise, for example the sound of traffic on a nearby road. The trick here is to plant the hedge as close to the source of the noise as possible, it will absorb the sounds and make the garden beyond a much quieter place.

Thirdly, hedges provide valuable shelter for wildlife in the garden. Birds will nest there, and hedgehogs and other small mammals will make their homes at the base. A wide range of spiders, insects and caterpillars will colonise the hedge; these are not only valuable food for garden birds, but may also be predators that eat garden pests, or important pollinators helping to set good crops of fruit and berries for autumn colour. Finally a well grown and tended hedge is a fine ornament to any garden, it has, to my mind, more character than a solid fence or wall, changing with the weather and the seasons. It can be shaped and clipped to fit the needs of the garden and the gardener, it can even be a different shape and size from one year to the next.

Obviously the species planted will affect the appearance and the wildlife content of a hedge, but there are so many different hedging plants to choose from, evergreen and deciduous, that there should be species to suit every taste. Avoid vigorous growers such as leyland cypress like the plague, and choose from beech, yew, holly, hawthorn, blackthorn, box, or hornbeam. Mix in roses, raspberries, red and blackcurrants, and hedgerow trees such as rowan, cherry, apple and damson for a tapestry of colours and textures.

Rhubarb

The end of October and the beginning of November are good times to plant soft fruits such as raspberries, blackcurrants and gooseberries. This also applies to rhubarb, though strictly speaking it is not a fruit but a leaf stalk or stem. *The Vegetable Growers Handbook,* by Arthur J. Simons, a Penguin handbook published just after the war, states that: "Rhubarb is seldom treated with sufficient respect!" and goes on to suggest that: "the recent surfeit of rhubarb accompanied by the shortage of fresh fruit, has probably sickened many people of it for the rest of their lives!" Be that as it may, rhubarb was obviously more popular than nowadays – he lists no fewer than eight named varieties and talks of planting three different ones on his vegetable plot to maintain successional cropping.

Today most people are either rhubarb lovers or rhubarb haters; if you are a fan, then 'crowns' of rhubarb should be planted now. They prefer a sunny position, allowing 3-4 feet between them and any other plants to avoid overshadowing. Dig in plenty of manure or rotted compost (Mr Simons recommends wood ash and bonemeal too). It is advisable not to harvest any stalks in the first year but to let the plants build up their strength. Neither should they be allowed to flower, cut off any flower spikes that form and mulch generously each spring with manure, compost or grass clippings.

Stems may be harvested from the second year onwards,

gently pulling them from the plant as soon as they are large enough to use. Rhubarb forcing is a traditional art – there are several approved methods, involving covering a rhubarb plant with a large pot, bucket or crate around midwinter time. This is then covered with a layer of leaves, straw or manure to exclude all light and to act as insulation from the worst of the cold weather. The resulting stems, which can be eaten from February onwards, are a bright, magenta pink, and very tasty! Plants forced in this way will require a year off before they can be harvested again. Rhubarb freezes well, and makes excellent pies and fruit fools (yes, I am a fan of rhubarb). There are numerous recipes for jams, preserves and wines.

Jobs for October

❀ Lift bedded out begonias while still in leaf, put in boxes in a dry shed or greenhouse to dry out and die back gradually. Remember to label them or note the colours to aid planting out next year

❀ Remove summer bedding and replace with winter and spring flowers such as wallflowers and winter pansies. Interplant with tulip and daffodil bulbs for a really full spring display.

❀ Empty out hanging baskets and containers as they go over. Plant with ivies, primulas and winter pansies as they become available.

❀ Pot lily bulbs into large pots, five or six in each, and overwinter them in a greenhouse or frost free shed. They will make excellent patio plants for next summer.

❀ Begin cutting down and tidying up herbaceous plants now. They are beginning to die back, and are easier to deal with before the rain and frosts make them slimy and mushy. Dig up and split any overgrown or large clumps, then replant smaller pieces after adding garden compost or rotted manure to the soil.

❀ Plant trees and shrubs between October and March. Prepare the ground thoroughly, digging it over and working in some organic matter, compost or manure. Remember to water them in well if the weather is dry.

❀ Plant new hedges; smaller plants will generally establish more quickly than larger ones, provided the soil is in good heart and they are kept well weeded.

❀ Begin the thankless task of raking fallen leaves from lawns and paths. Storing the leaves in a compost bin, to rot down and make leaf mould, may make the job more satisfying.

❀ Remove fallen leaves from ponds and pools before they begin to rot and pollute the water.

❀ Check gutters and drains are not blocked by leaves, to avoid unexpected floods.

November

November can be quite a shock to the system! Cold, wet weather often coupled with high winds means that there are few visitors to the gardens. We begin our winter tasks and projects, in between sweeping up fallen leaves, unblocking gutters and drains, and providing holly and other evergreens to decorate the house in time for the annual Craft Fair. The sheep arrive, rare-breeds such as Shetland, North Ronaldsay and Boreray, courtesy of Jennie Hill at Greenholme in Penrith. They will spend the winter grazing the wildflower meadow, discouraging woody weeds and breaking up the turf; it's like welcoming back old friends!

Gardening for wildlife

There is often a perception that 'wildlife friendly' gardens are slightly untidy places, filled with native plants and hence not particularly colourful. Having attended a five-day course at the Snowdonia National Park Study Centre, entitled 'Wildlife enhancement in historic gardens and parklands', I am pleased to tell you that this need not be so!

The course focused on wild and garden plants used together in tandem, to provide year round food and cover for wildlife of all shapes and sizes, from tiny soil organisms, to beetles, birds and hedgehogs. There were plenty of new ideas and thoughts to absorb, many of them from fellow members of the course (who included several National Trust gardeners, a park ranger from Ipswich and two staff from the RHS gardens at Wisley.) I have been putting several of these new concepts into practise at Brockhole; here are my top ten topical hints on how to make *your* garden more wildlife friendly without sacrificing colour or horticultural standards:

☺ Plant ornamental shrubs, such as cotoneaster, rowan, hawthorn, shrub roses and berberis, which have autumn and winter hips, haws and berries. These are extremely valuable food for birds and will encourage them to visit your garden.

☺ Build some wooden compost bins and fill them with garden rubbish and lawn clippings. Not only will this make useful compost for your garden, it will also be a habitat for fungi and little insects; placing a large pipe in the bottom of the heap will provide a snug winter refuge for hedgehogs. The heat generated may even encourage grass snakes to make their home with you.

☺ Make a tidy log or brash pile from tree or shrub prunings. Left to weather naturally in an out-of-the-way corner, this will become a haven for invertebrates, fungi and ferns. Wrens often nest in such piles and other birds will feed on the insects there.

☺ There are many ornamental shrubs and herbaceous plants, such as *Calamintha*, *Buddleia*, *Aquliegia*, *Erigeron*, *Aster*, *Filipendula* and *Sedum* that are excellent nectar sources. Mixing them into your borders, amongst your existing plants, will encourage butterflies to feed in your garden.

☺ If you can bear to, grow a small nettle or thistle patch in a sunny spot to provide food for the caterpillars of moths and butterflies.

☺ Grow flowering plants such as *Helianthemum*, *Hypericum*, *Hebe* and *Verbascum*, which are attractive to bees and hover-flies.

☺ Plants with ornamental seed heads will attract seed-eating birds, including greenfinches and goldfinches. Remember to leave the seed heads on well into the winter months, to give the birds plenty of time to eat all the seeds.

☺ Allow a patch of ivy to flower each winter, to provide food for bees, flies and other insects, and shelter for small birds such as wrens.

☺ Plants such as evening primrose and candytuft, that attract moths, will also attract bats. They may roost in nearby buildings or large trees, or even your garden shed!

☺ Keep a wildlife diary and record which animals and insects have been visiting. Noting which plants and areas of the garden they have been using may help with future planning and planting, and will remind you why you left that patch of nettles in the first place!

Gardening or birding?

Now that the cold and miserable winter weather has arrived, and we have begun to wrap up warmly to work outside, it is time to think of those other visitors to the garden, the birds. All spring and summer they have graced our gardens with their cheerful presence and enthusiastic song; now it is our turn to give them a helping hand as the harsh winter months begin to make things difficult for them.

We can start by putting out feeding stations for them, with supplies of fat, suet, peanuts, sunflower seeds and other high-energy scraps. These will attract greenfinches, chaffinches, bluetits, great-tits, nuthatches and perhaps, if you are lucky, greater spotted woodpeckers. These smartly coloured birds make up for the lack of floral colour in the winter garden with room to spare as far as I'm concerned!

I was interested to read in a bird magazine that our resident garden birds are joined each winter by many migrants from Scandinavia and Europe. It is fascinating to think that the robin or blackbird on your bird table may have travelled thousands of miles to breakfast in your garden. A supply of fresh, unfrozen water is of particular importance to birds for drinking and bathing. If you have a pond or pool this will attract birds, and if your garden is a long way from a river or other reliable source of water it would be helpful to put out a shallow container of water for them.

There are many plants that we can grow to provide food and shelter for garden birds during the winter months. Berberis and cotoneaster spring instantly to mind, many birds enjoy the profusion of berries that they provide. Other shrubs with edible berries include elder, hollies, pyracantha, roses and rowan. Windfall apples and pears will attract blackbirds and thrushes, and also redwings and fieldfares if the winter is particularly harsh and they have exhausted supplies of hedgerow berries, so don't be in too much of a hurry to clear them up. Mistle thrushes are very partial to yew berries, and the jays at Brockhole are feasting now on acorns, as well as storing some away for later use.

Beech mast is enjoyed by ground feeding birds such as pheasants.

For many years, I have grown teasels in the garden to attract the finches. By the time I cleared away the old flower stems each winter I was disappointed that I had not seen any birds feeding on the seed-heads. Then, one year, I was late with my tidying up, and there in January and February were little flocks of goldfinches eating teasel seeds! It pays not to be too quick to tidy up! Birds will feed on the seed-heads of many plants such as ornamental grasses, sunflowers, verbascum or mullein, golden rod, lavender, and red-hot-pokers. The ornamental members of the thistle family such as globe artichoke, the globe thistle or *Echinops*, and cardoons, are all useful stocks of edible food for seed-eating birds.

Lawns are a larder full of food for birds such as starlings, thrushes and blackbirds, which will feed on worms, leatherjackets and other insects, provided pesticides have not been used. I feel that a few worm casts, easily brushed away before mowing, are a small price to pay for the sight of a blackbird, its head cocked on one side, running across the lawn in search of a meal. Finally we must remember the smaller insect eating birds such as robins and wrens. An old wall covered with thick climbers such as ivy or honeysuckle will provide a haven for spiders, woodlice and other overwintering invertebrates, the perfect food for little birds, together with a sheltered spot in which to eat them!

Tree inspections

Many of the trees at Brockhole are over a hundred years old, planted when the gardens and grounds were landscaped by Thomas Mawson; some are older, they may already have been sizeable specimens when Mawson began his work. In recent years I have generally spent a day or two every autumn with Alex Todd, the National Park's Forestry Foreman, looking at the health, or otherwise, of these larger trees. Autumn is a good time for tree inspections, any fungi that are infecting their roots, butts or branches may well be producing fruiting bodies (mushrooms,

Abies concolor

toadstools or bracket fungus to you and I) giving a clue that all is not well inside the tree.

So we stalk around the tree bases, looking as if we have lost the car keys but really searching for basal and root-rot fungi; and we stare up into the branches as if we have seen a strange bird or a UFO, on the lookout for bracket fungi and deadwood. Occasionally we find indications that all is not well and a long discussion usually follows. We have to decide whether we should fell the tree, remove some of the crown, take out the decaying wood or simply monitor the health of the tree for another 12 months. It all depends on the type of tree and the type of fungus or structural problem. Much depends also on the position of the tree; what is acceptable in an area of woodland where few people ever go is quite different from what is acceptable in the car park area or at the adventure playground.

We have begun tagging the trees with individual numbers. These little aluminium tags (fastened with aluminium nails so as not to harm the trees) will help us to keep track of each individual specimen; eventually I hope to make a database of numbered trees, species, girth, height, work done on them etc. etc. For the moment, they will be useful for recording Alex's comments and our joint decisions, ensuring that the right work is done on the right trees, a few weeks or months down the line.

Visitors to the Gardeners' building have been surprised by the open space that has appeared next to the garage. In a burst of enthusiasm we have removed a huge *Rhododendron ponticum*, (not a very politically correct plant to be growing in the National Park) which had grown up from the rootstock of a rhododendron hybrid long since perished. In the spring, when the soil has settled and rested we will be planting the gap with some more horticulturally interesting specimens such as *Embothrium*, *Eucryphia* and *Enkianthus*.

Planting new trees

One of the most satisfying sights for the gardener must surely be young trees planted in previous years. Sometimes it is easy to feel that they are such a long-term commitment that one should not expect to see any appreciable difference in size from one year to the next. But after only a few years growth there begins to appear a plant of significant proportions, and to have been the instigator of this growth can be a matter of great pride. There are trees at Brockhole that I planted in the first few years after becoming Head Gardener, which are now between 20 and 30 feet high. The thought that in another 50 to 60 years they will be mighty trees has often sustained me when I am planting the current year's crop of small trees in cold and dreary winter weather.

There are several decisions to make before planting a tree in the garden, the most important of which must surely be the species of tree itself. It is no use planting a birch or rowan if you have plenty of space and you want your descendants to appreciate it in 150 years time. Equally, it is no use planting an oak or beech in a small back garden so that it has to be felled in 20 years when its roots begin to undermine the house! Look up your choices in a textbook or catalogue, or ask for advice at the garden centre or nursery if you're not sure. In addition to size and longevity, you may also want to take into consideration ornamental blossom, autumn colour, fruits, the amount of shade cast, and whether you prefer a deciduous tree or a conifer.

The size of the tree when it is planted is the next thing to consider. Whilst it is true that planting a large tree will give a much more immediate effect, it is also true that a small tree will almost always catch up in size within a few years, and will often produce a stronger and better shaped tree in the end. The other advantage in planting small is financial; a large "heavy standard" may set you back several hundred pounds, whilst a one or two year old "whip" may only be a few pence.

Now to the matter of planting time. Generally, deciduous trees are best planted between mid-autumn and mid-spring. Conifers are best planted in early spring, whilst pot or container grown trees can be planted at any time of the year provided careful attention is paid to regular watering. In all cases, trees should not be planted in frosty weather or if the ground is water-logged. Having acquired your tree and decided when and where to plant it, next dig the hole. The planting hole should be about three times as large as the rootball of the tree, and one and half times as deep. Work some organic matter into the base and mix a little more with the soil taken out of the hole. Do not be tempted to use peat for this, it is becoming a scarce resource and in any case, unlike well-rotted compost or manure, it contains no nutrients useful to the tree. Fork over the base of the hole and make sure the sides are not smooth.

A tree with a small rootball in proportion to its height, or any tree over about five feet tall, may require staking. It has been shown that short stakes, which allow the bulk of the tree to sway slightly and thus encourage the growth of anchoring roots, are more effective than taller stakes. Drive the stake in to one side of the hole before placing the tree beside it. Backfill with the excavated soil ensuring that the finished level is the same as it was when the tree was in its pot or in the nursery (there will be a mark on the trunk where it was touching the soil). Tread the soil down firmly and fasten the tree to its stake with a plastic or rubber tree tie and spacer.

Thick mulch or a mulch mat will prevent competition from weeds and help to prevent the soil from drying out. Water new trees copiously in dry weather and check ties and stakes every few months to ensure they are not rubbing on the trunk or branches. And in a few years you will be able to look up a your hard work and realise that it was all worth while!

Shrubs for autumn colour

In true November 5th style, there are some shrubs and trees that will light up your garden as brightly as any bonfire, their leaves have such brilliant autumn colour that they seem almost to be alight!

I'm sure I have mentioned *Enkianthus campanulatus* before, but I make no apology for drawing your attention to it again. Along with the katsura tree, *Cercidiphyllum japonicum*, it has the most brilliant autumn colour that I know of. Both are easy to grow, the first having creamy white, heather-like flowers in spring and the second having new leaves that are an attractive bronze at the beginning of the year. The fallen leaves of *Cercidiphyllum* are supposed to smell of burnt toffee, but I can't say I have ever noticed them.

Almost all of the Japanese maples have bright autumn colour, as does a little known relative of the witch hazel, *Fothergilla major*. This unassuming shrub has tufts of deliciously fragrant white flowers in spring and excellent red, orange and yellow leaf colour in the autumn. Incidentally there is one species of witch hazel, *Hamamelis virginiana*, that flowers in late autumn, its fragrant, spidery yellow flowers are a welcome addition to the autumn colour in the garden. Another relative of the witch hazel

Vitis coignetiae – a climber with excellent autumn colour

is *Disanthus cercidifolius*, a plant that I have been growing for several years now. It is a small shrub, very slow growing, and with inconspicuous blue-green, heart-shaped leaves. It has spectacular autumn leaf colour, and small, dark red flowers that appear after leaf fall, looking like pairs of back-to-back spiders!

Euonymus, the spindle bushes, used to be widely planted in parks and larger gardens. They are less often seen these days, perhaps because they are not very interesting in spring and summer. They have the most brilliant red autumn foliage however, coupled with unusual fruits often in the most bizarre colour combinations. *Euonymus europaeus* has red fruits opening to reveal orange seeds, *E. japonicus* has pink fruits and orange seeds, whilst the winged spindle *E. alatus* has purple and red fruits.

Back-ache

If like me you suffer from a bad back, then gardening, however much we love to do it, can quite literally be a pain. Over the past few years I have discovered, through experience and through talking to fellow sufferers, some useful ways of coping with gardening without too much grief. The most important tip is to do little and often, rather than trying to work for hours on end. It's better to do an hour or so at a time and keep on top of things than to let them build up into a large task. The second most important thing is to enlist help whenever possible. Keep a list of those awkward jobs in mind, so that the next time someone asks if you'd like a hand with anything, you can use their help to its best advantage.

My favourite piece of gardening equipment these days is a pair of tough waterproof overtrousers! I find it much more comfortable to do low level pruning, edging and weeding whilst kneeling down, and the trousers keep my knees dry and relatively warm. Getting up again afterwards can be more of a problem, a strategically placed spade or garden fork to lean on can be helpful! Long-handled tools to avoid the need to bend are an absolute must. I have had my favourite border spade fitted with an extra long handle, I also make use of hoes (though these can involve pushing and twisting which is painful for some) and a little hand fork on a long shaft. Garden Centres now stock litter pickers, cunning devices with pincers at the end, originally designed for picking up litter, but equally useful for picking up clippings and prunings without bending.

I was recently introduced to flower arrangers' secateurs and scissors. These cut through stems like normal secateurs, but hold on to the cutting afterwards until they are reopened. I have found these invaluable as it means that I do not have to lean forward with both arms, one to hold the stem and one to cut it. Nor do I have to pick up clippings from the ground, I can cut them and deposit them in a basket or bucket with just one hand.

Wheelbarrows can be particularly awkward to use if you suffer from back pain, involving not only lifting but pushing as well. If I have to use one I will try to split the load and make two or three journeys instead of one, and to place the load as closely above the wheel as possible. This puts the weight on to the wheel rather than on to my arms and back. An excellent alternative is a sack barrow. Granted it will not carry the same loads as a wheelbarrow, but with a little ingenuity a sack-barrow can be used to carry buckets of weeds or compost, sacks of fertiliser and potting medium, and all manner of pots and containers, without the need for lifting. A sturdy sack-barrow with fat pneumatic tyres is

best for use on rough ground; those with solid wheels are only for use on smooth floors and paving. A wide platform is also a must, mine is a bit too narrow and some containers will not balance on it.

Finally, let us consider mowing the lawn. A powered mower is a very useful piece of machinery, where the engine powers the wheels as well as the blades, thus involving no pushing on the part of the operator. Emptying the grass box is probably the next worse bit; it should be emptied often before it becomes too heavy and awkward. In warm, dry weather I might cut without using the box at all; if you mow regularly, while the grass is still relatively short, the clippings will not be much of a nuisance if left on the surface to dry out and disperse naturally.

A *Westmorland Gazette* reader sent me some more useful hints for bad-back sufferers – the suggestion that we spend time "warming up" with a few stretching exercises before embarking on a stint of gardening is an excellent one. Joggers, swimmers, football players and all manner of other athletes use this technique to ease muscles and joints into action, so why not gardeners?

Jobs for November

❀ Plant spring-flowering bulbs such as tulips, daffodils and alliums. Plant hyacinths and minature daffodils in pots to flower indoors.

❀ Take a close look at any 'background' plants in your garden. Are there any hedges, laurels, ivy, rhododendron or hollies that have surreptitiously grown to cover more space than was originally intended? Now is a good time to cut them back.

❀ Shorten any long shoots on rose bushes, to prevent strong winds from rocking them and damaging the root system.

❀ If the ground is dry enough, give your lawn a final cut. After mowing give your mower a really thorough clean down and store it in a dry garage or shed for the winter. Send it off for servicing if necessary.

❀ Rake fallen leaves carefully from beneath roses and any other shrubs that have suffered from mildew, blackspot or other fungal diseases. Burn these leaves to destroy overwintering fungal spores.

❀ Lift dahlias as soon as the foliage has been blackened by frost. Clean up the tubers and store them in a dry, frost-free shed or greenhouse.

❀ A good mulch of manure or well rotted compost around the base of climbers will help to stimulate strong new growths next year.

❀ Plant lily bulbs in the garden at a depth of two to three times the height of the bulb. Add grit and leaf mould to the soil to encourage strong growth.

❀ Prune or clip any remaining deciduous hedges, such as hawthorn, blackthorn or beech. Holly hedges can be cut now too.

❀ Cut down on the watering and feeding of conservatory plants now that light levels and outside temperatures are lower.

December

The end of the year, and the chance to relax slightly and take stock of the seasons gone by. With each passing year, I learn a little bit more about gardening and plants, and with each year I realise how little I really know and how much there is left to learn. No-one can hope to know everything about a subject a huge and as idiosyncratic as the plant world.
The nights draw in and we have to wait for the sun to rise before we can emerge from the tea room each morning, by three o'clock it's twilight again!

Winter flowers

There may be some patches of flowers, left over from the summer, still hanging on in the garden; odd rose blooms, a few cyclamen, a chrysanthemum or two. But these are summer's left-overs, not true winter flowering plants, and most of the colour in the winter garden has to be provided by evergreen shrubs, either with variegated leaves or with colourful berries. There are how-ever a handful of plants whose true flowering time is during the winter months, and it is well worth considering giving these a place on your plot for the pleasure of seeing fresh flowers in December.

A plant familiar to me from my childhood, which my mother grows close to the back door so that she can easily pick sprays for the house, is winter jasmine, *Jasminum nudiflorum*. A native of China, it is a rather straggly plant, best grown against a wall or over a fence. The flowers are produced before the leaves, hence the Latin name *nudiflorum*; they are a bright, canary yellow which contrasts well with the dark green of the shoots. The plant can get a bit straggly or full of old, non-flowering wood, this is easily remedied by cutting it back hard in Spring giving it plenty of time to produce new shoots to flower the following winter,

Another of my favourites is the viburnum. There are three or four species which flower during the winter; the best known are

Viburnum tinus and *Viburnum x bodnantense.* The first is an evergreen shrub from the Mediterranean; it bears clusters of pink and white flowers throughout the winter and is a useful plant for flower arranging. However its flowers are nowhere near as charming as those of *V.x bodnantense.* This is a deciduous shrub, and its flowers are borne on the bare wood of winter; they are white, delicately flushed with pink, and as an added bonus they are heavily scented. It is a plant of garden origin, being the hybrid of two wild Chinese species.

The Christmas rose, *Helleborus niger,* is a perennial plant that should, according to its name, be flowering in December, but if the weather is very cold it will often delay until the New Year. The elegant, saucer-shaped flowers, often up to 3 inches across, are white with greenish-white centres, ageing to pinkish white. Slugs are as fond of the flowers as gardeners, and should be kept at bay if possible. The plants may give up flowering if left in the same place for too long; I like to dig them up and divide them every few years, adding some leaf mould or well -rotted compost to the soil before replanting.

For many years there has been a rhododendron at Brockhole named 'Christmas Cheer', and in all the time I have worked there it has never flowered until late January at the earliest! Next to it however, is another rhododendron called *Rhododendron nobleanum,* which flowers reliably every December. Trusses of rose pink, tubular flowers are produced during spells of mild weather from late autumn to early spring. I am never quite sure if it is the last rhododendron to flower, or the first; perhaps it is both!

Time Management

A while ago I went on a day-course on Time Management. A strange choice you might think, and not really in keeping with the traditional idea of the Gardener, who should have all the time in the world for both the mundane and the time-consuming skilled jobs that arise in his or her daily work. Sadly for me, and for most other professional gardeners, this is no longer true, and like everyone else in the modern world we must find the most efficient and cost effective ways of working. In truth there never seems to be enough time to get round to all the jobs that need doing!

Hence the course on Time Management. There were lots of useful ideas talked about, but the one that sticks in my memory, and which I am trying to put into practise, was one called 'sharpening the saw'. The snappy illustration that introduced the idea was a picture of a man trying to cut down a tree with a blunt saw. His mate comes past and asks him why he doesn't stop to sharpen the saw so making his job easier. The man, who has been sawing for several hours, says he is too busy to stop – he has to finish sawing down this tree!

You see the idea? He needs to take a step back from the job in hand, do some maintenance or preparatory work, which will then make the original task much easier, quicker and more pleasant! This idea can be applied to loads of gardening jobs when you stop and think about it, especially if you are slightly untidy or disorganised as I am. For instance; how much time have you spent searching for a pair of secateurs or a particular trowel or fork, in order to do a job that would have taken only a few minutes? An hour or so on a rainy afternoon spent tidying the tool cupboard, a few minutes at the end of every gardening session to clean tools and put them away in the right place, and the frustration and wasted time of lost tools need never occur.

Another for instance; it can be a real struggle to trim overgrown grass edges that have become squashed by the mower or by passing feet. Some time spent with a half-moon cutter, or even better installing a metal edge, would make the weekly edge trimming almost a pleasure. And here's one I am particularly prone to; I don't have the time to plan, grow and plant out something to fill that empty space in the border, I'm too busy keeping it weeded! If I took time to fill the space with plants and then to mulch the whole area, then the plants and the mulch would do the weeding for me and I would have time to do something else, or even time to stand back and admire my handiwork!

Unless you really are an old-fashioned gardener with plenty of time on your hands, or unless you are already well practised in time management, there are lots of instances where you can put these ideas into practise. Wearing the right clothes when you go out into the garden – not being too hot or having fingers too cold to do the job comfortably; using the correct tools for the job; maintaining your tools in good condition; marking where you have planted bulbs to prevent digging them up by mistake; preparing the soil before making new plantings; and so on and so on!

I haven't got it down to a fine art yet, and I still find myself taking too long over some jobs through lack of sufficient planning, but I'm working on it. Now if I could find my course notes I could tell you what other hot tips I picked up!

Common polypody and maidenhair spleenwort

Commemorative fruit trees

To anyone thinking of planting a tree to commemorate a family event, may I make a plea for the humble fruit tree? Generally it seems people choose between a large stately tree such as an oak or beech, and a smaller, more ornamental tree such as flowering

cherry or rowan. But there are many points in favour of planting an apple tree, or a pear, or plum tree ....

Firstly, because they are fruit trees, they will produce flowers in the spring. This means they will be looking good early in the year – the first apple blossom is always a treat after the drab days of winter. Secondly, the fruits themselves can be quite ornamental. The changing shape and colours of apples and pears as they grow and ripen are worthy of note, the rich purple of ripening plums is the essence of autumn colour.

Thirdly, there is always the possibility of some kind of crop, though I will admit that Cumbria is not a county renowned for its fruit growing. Having said that, where would we be without the Lyth Valley damsons? Spectacular blossoming in spring and a wonderful fruit crop most autumns, with damson jam, pies and gin to look forward to! One of my proudest possessions at Brockhole is a small damson tree that grows at the centre of the herb garden. It came as a cutting from a tree in the Lyth Valley, and this autumn proudly produced its first two damsons. What a taste of things to come!

Because they respond well to pruning, and because they can be grafted onto growth restricting rootstocks, fruit trees such as apples and pears can be grown in the smallest of spaces. My mother grows an apple tree (on dwarfing rootstock) in a large pot, where it flowers and fruits just as handsomely as its larger cousins. They can be grown happily against walls and fences, and trained as espaliers, cordons and many other fancy shapes. Fruit trees are great for encouraging birds, bees and other insects into the garden. The early blossom is a blessing for emerging insect life in spring, and windfall apples and pears are a valuable food source for butterflies and birds such as thrushes and blackbirds.

Finally, if well looked after in their early years, fruit trees can live to a great age. Granted they would be unlikely to reach the next millennium, but then not many trees other than yews will do that! They could certainly last well over 100 years and so be around for several future generations to appreciate.

Christmas flowers

During Christmas week it has become a habit of mine to walk around the gardens at Brockhole to see how many flowers I can count. Admittedly many of these are rather bedraggled, and some are only a couple of rogue flowers produced when the rest of the plant has long since given up flowering, but nevertheless I have counted up to 26 plants in flower!

Penstemon 'Sour Grapes'

Some plants are at the end of their flowering period, such as the kaffir lily, *Schizostylis coccinea* and the penstemon 'Hidcote Pink'. Some plants are just beginning to come into flower, like the witch hazels or *Hamamelis,* and *Helleborus x sternii,* whose flowers really belong to January or February. Some plants such as rosemary and some tough little purple hebes (that I have long since forgotten the name for) seem to be flowering whatever time of year I look at them.

Other plants, however, are flowering because this is when they are supposed to flower! One of the most surprising is the eucalyptus or gum tree, which I received with the name of *Eucalyptus vernicosa,* although I can't find this name in any of my textbooks. It has little clusters of fluffy white flowers nestling amongst the silvery green leaves – quite charming! Eucalyptus can be awkward to grow as trees in English gardens, they tend to grow very quickly and the soft woody stems bend easily, so that the resulting tree is not a good shape. They have both juvenile and adult foliage; the young leaves are generally more attractive than the old, but are replaced almost entirely by adult foliage as the tree matures. The answer to both these habits is to grow the Eucalyptus as shrubs, cutting them back hard as growth begins in Spring, thus keeping the plant a manageable size whilst also encouraging the production of juvenile foliage. I should mention that this is a practise fraught with danger, and for every successful pruning I have managed, I have killed another gum tree by pruning too late, or too early, or on a Monday instead of on a Thursday, or for some other unfathomable reason.

Lonicera purpusii 'Winter Beauty' blooms in December; it is an insignificant looking, shrubby honeysuckle that bears tubular white flowers with yellow stamens. It would be quite easy to walk past this plant and fail to notice that it was flowering, except that the flowers have the most delicious scent that stops you in your tracks and demands that you look for the source of the fragrance! Last, but definitely not least of the winter flowers, I should mention mahonia. There are several different species and cultivars of mahonia, all of which have large clusters of bright yellow flowers and many of which flower at this time of year. One of the best is *Mahonia x media*, some varieties of which have flower spikes up to 18 inches long! The plants have handsome, large, dark green leaves that make an attractive architectural feature when they are not in bloom. They can grow quite tall if left to their own devices; to keep them under control, and to keep the foliage as large as possible, it is advisable to cut around one third of the oldest stems back hard directly flowering has finished.

Presents for gardeners

Perhaps because Christmas falls in a quiet time in the gardening calendar, it is easy to forget to give horticultural Christmas gifts to those of our friends and relations who are keen gardeners. Here is my top ten list of the perfect presents for anyone who would rather be out in the garden than eating too much turkey whilst watching "The Great Escape" on TV again!

Top of the pile is a pair of secateurs. Not just any secateurs but a pair of Felco secateurs. Made in Switzerland, these will last a lifetime and give satisfaction with every cut! They are expensive, selling at around £40, but no serious gardener should be seen with anything else. Felco also make secateurs for left-handed people. Another very useful tool is a small pruning saw. These come in a range of sizes, with prices ranging from £5 to around £15; they are used to cut small branches too big for secateurs but not big enough to need a bow saw. The models that fold up are especially useful, as they can be carried in a pocket for use at a moment's notice!

A good quality, stainless steel knife is something that can be of use to the gardener; I tend to use mine mostly for preparing cuttings. Knives are quite a personal choice, so if you are wanting to buy one for someone else it might be best to take the recipient with you to choose their own. A new watering can is a real luxury! There are loads to choose from but it's generally the case that you get what you pay for. Haws make the best cans in my opinion, strong and well balanced, they are now made in light plastic as well as the traditional galvanised steel. The brass roses come in a range of spray sizes for watering everything from the most delicate of seedlings to the most beefy of pot plants.

An electric propagator is something that many gardeners would like but feel they can't quite justify or afford; which makes them great presents. Again there is plenty of choice, from large, greenhouse models right down to mini-propagators that will sit on a windowsill. The gentle heat they provide will help with the germination of seedlings and the rooting of cuttings. A small portable potting bench is a good present for anyone who has to do their potting at the kitchen table. These are moulded plastic, with a back and sides to stop the compost falling off, small enough to sit on a table or wide shelf when in use and light enough to hang on the wall when not needed.

Once you have used stainless steel tools it is difficult to be satisfied with any other sort, they are so much easier and more efficient to use, not to mention easier to keep clean and longer lasting. Spoil your gardening friends with a stainless steel fork, spade or trowel and they will be your friends forever! Packets of seeds and small tools such as dibbers make good tree or cracker presents, and most gardeners that I know would be delighted to receive a new plant or houseplant for Christmas. Oddly enough, hardly anyone ever gives keen gardeners bunches of flowers as presents, something they of all people would appreciate, especially if the bunch had some unusual flowers in it.

Finally, gardening books; great for reference during the growing season or for browsing through when the weather is too bad to be out. If I had to pick only one from the dozens available it would be the Royal Horticultural Society's 'Encyclopaedia of Gardening'.

Christmas decorations

Not being a great one for loads of artificial decorations, I like to decorate our rooms at home with garden flowers, fruits and foliage at Christmas time. Each year I bring in armfuls of cuttings from the garden, to make big, generally spiky, and definitely seasonal arrangements in vases and jugs throughout the house. In order to be truly traditional, I generally include some Christmas roses and a little holly and ivy in these decorations. After that, tradition is thrown to the winds, and anything that is looking good in the garden is invited in for sherry and mince pies.

I start with the ornamental stems of dogwood and willow, in shades of deep red, bright green and orange-yellow. To these, I add the rich red foliage of *Photinia* 'Red Robin' and the creamy foliage of variegated *Pittosporum*. A branch or two of *Eucalyptus* gives a subtle scent and a blue-grey tint that looks lovely next to the red flowers of *Rhododendron nobleanum*. (This early flowered rhododendron always flowers during December, making up for the disappointment of its neighbour, *Rhododendron* 'Christmas Cheer' which never begins flowering until January with us!) Some of the brightest of fruits to be included in my Christmas arrangements are those of *Iris foetidissima*. The cylindrical seedpods gently split in the warmth of the house to reveal bright orange seeds within. Occasionally I put the violet berries of *Callicarpa bodinieri* in the same vase, but generally it seems best to keep them in separate arrangements!

The tiny flowers of *Sarcococcus* are deliciously scented, as are the flowers of the various species of witch hazel, though I will be lucky to find these flowering before early January. Also pleasantly perfumed are the flowers of *Viburnum bodnantense* and those of the winter-flowering honeysuckle, *Lonicera purpusii* 'Winter Beauty'. The red berries of *Skimmia japonica* echo those of the holly, and can be used in contrast to the white and pink berries of *Pernettya*. The catkins of *Garrya* and hazel, the broad, spear-shaped leaves of New Zealand flax, the cones of larch and alder, the twisted stems of corkscrew hazel and *Corokia;* the list of candidates goes on and on. Each year the arrangements are different, depending on what is available and what the weather has been like, but each year they brighten the house and give a small hint that if Christmas is here now, then spring can't be too far behind!

Jobs for December

❀ Keep an eye out for fungal diseases in the greenhouse and treat with fungicide if necessary. Try to keep a flow of air movement if possible — open a window during the day or run a small fan heater on a cool setting.

❀ Check greenhouses and frames for lost, loose or broken panes. Make repairs as soon as possible, the next lot of high winds may get in through these gaps and do much more damage.

❀ Clean the leaves of houseplants with a little milk or a proprietary leaf shine. With the low light levels at this time of year, they need all the help they can get.

❀ Send off seed orders or purchase seeds for next year from the garden centre. Don't leave it too late — some of the more popular varieties may quickly be sold out.

❀ Protect any slightly tender plants from frost, with straw or bracken tucked around the base, or with horticultural fleece on top on nights when frost is forecast.

❀ Make sure that paths, and especially steps, do not become slippery in icy weather. Sprinkle a little salt on them to melt any frost or ice, but be careful not to use too much or it may wash onto the borders and damage your plants.

❀ Check stored bulbs and corms regularly for fungal diseases and damage by rodents.

❀ Look carefully at any larger or mature trees in your garden now that the leaves have fallen. Are there any dead or diseased branches that will need removing this winter?

❀ Cut the old flower spikes from Pampas grasses as they begin to fade and look tatty. Every couple of years I give the foliage of our plants a good haircut during the winter, to remove excess thatch.

❀ Check, and renew if necessary, ties on climbers and trees. Replace any rotten posts or stakes, or remove them if they are no longer needed.

Autobiography

Sue Tasker: Head Gardener at Brockhole

1

Although born in Ruislip, I grew up in Stockton-on Tees in the north-east of England. This is not an area renowned for the splendour of its gardens, but my father was a construction manager for ICI, so it was a sensible place for us to live. My two brothers, my sister and I went to local primary schools and later to the Grammar School and to Stockton Sixth Form College.

I don't remember being especially interested in plants whilst I was a child, though my brothers, sister and I all had our own small plots within my parents' garden. My mother was (and still is) in charge of plants and flowers, my father was (and still is) in charge of the lawns. They still live in the house where we grew up, despite efforts to persuade them to move to Cumbria where my younger brother and I both live.

What I do remember being interested in is the Lake District. My father had spent his childhood holidays at Seascale and Holmrook, where my grandfather, an electrical engineer from Lancashire, liked to fish. He has fond memories of the west coast before the days of Sellafield, when the original jetty still stood on the beach at Seascale. It seemed natural therefore that we should have holidays there too, and every summer for years my parents rented a flat in Rueberry House at the very end of Seascale village. It was a brilliant place for children, with steps from the garden, down the cliff, to the beach, and with miles of sand and rock pools to play with. Every couple of days we went walking, in Wasdale or Eskdale usually, and one day each year we went to Ambleside or Bowness for a meal and to spend our holiday pocket money.

The first plants I remember growing were some stems of goat or pussy willow that my Dad brought home. Arranged in a vase

of water, they soon grew roots, so I insisted on planting one in the garden. For years my poor mother had to put up with a large willow tree which, although decorative in spring, was generally covered with greenfly and sooty mould by midsummer! I have had a soft spot for willows ever since, but after I left home they dug it up and were glad to see the back of it! Another tree I bequeathed to my parents' garden, which is still growing there, was a silver birch. I remember going out to buy a sapling and being amused by the idea of paying for it by the foot. In my small plot I grew an eclectic selection of annuals, beetroot, lettuces and perennial cornflowers. I have a piece of the very same cornflower in a border at Brockhole, to remind me of home.

2

For a long time now there has been the perception that gardening, along with woodwork and cookery, is for those who do not excel at academic subjects, but with the added disadvantage that, unlike woodwork and cookery, it is seldom if ever taught in schools. This has become something of a self-fulfilling prophecy that few have tried to challenge or change; and brighter children are not encouraged to think about a career in horticulture. This was certainly the case for me, and over the years I have met many, many gardeners who have come to the profession later in life, after an aborted career in, for example, teaching, banking, the law, or engineering.

Certainly no-one at the Girls' Grammar School or the Sixth Form College that I went to ever suggested or even dreamt that I might be a budding horticulturalist, least of all me! If you were bright, you took 'O' levels, then 'A' levels and if you did well then you went on to college or university to study for as many qualifications as you could. Jobs were relatively easy to find in those days as long as you had the right pieces of paper to back you up. And so, in the autumn of 1974, armed with four shiny new 'A' levels, I set off for Manchester University to study for a BA in Human Geography.

I can't remember very much of my first and only year at university, perhaps having purposely forgotten the details, but I do remember being thoroughly miserable! I certainly missed my family and friends and did not enjoy the course as much as I should have done, and I am quite sure that it rained every single day for three terms. Not disciplined enough to study properly on my own with only a few weekly lectures and the odd tutorial to guide me, I spent long hours wandering through art galleries, second hand bookshops and round the city parks. The only useful thing I did was to learn to drive, in a red BSM mini, in rush hour, city traffic. Failing my driving test but passing my first-year exams by the skin of my teeth, I packed my things and left.

I have never regretted leaving, promising myself never again to stay anywhere where I was so unhappy, but fortunately I have never had to put this to the test. There is a great deal to be said for taking a year or two 'out' before going on to further education; it might have given me a chance to grow up a bit more, and perhaps sort out what I really wanted to do with my life. A small part of me is slightly niggled at not having finished my degree, and over the intervening years I have slowly been working towards an Open University degree. At my current rate, it will only take another ten or twelve years!

3

As an antidote to my unsuccessful attempt at further education, I went to live with and work for some friends, Muriel and David Passey, at their home in the depths of the North Yorkshire countryside. Their garden was old, rambling, slightly unkempt but oozing with charm. They had no other gardener and I made my way by a mixture of advice from David and Muriel, by reading as many gardening books as I could lay my hands on and by learning from my mistakes!

Muriel taught me my first Latin plant names and passed on to me her love for old-fashioned roses. She helped me to pass my driving test, took me beagling and to point-to-point races, round Anglo-Saxon churches and the streets of medieval York. David taught me the finer points of vegetable growing, tree planting and glazing greenhouses, and how to work from dawn until dusk in the pouring rain. Between them they gave me back my self-confidence and showed me that a career in horticulture might be the thing for me.

When I left Manchester to take up gardening, I had promised my parents that I would try to get some kind of horticultural qualifications. Having already used up a years worth of my student grant, I was interested to read about a three year student course at the Royal Botanic Gardens Kew, where students were paid a wage whilst they studied. Applicants had to have 2 'A' levels and to have worked in horticulture for at least two years before applying; it seemed ideal. There was just one snag, there were only 22 places each year and competition was fierce.

Without much hope, but with plenty of enthusiasm, I sent off my application form to Kew. You may imagine my surprise, and slight panic, when I received an official letter asking me to attend an interview. My memory of this interview, together with my first visit to Kew, is extremely vague. I must have done something right however, because a couple of weeks later I received another official letter informing me that I had been given a place on Course 16 of the Kew Diploma in Horticulture, beginning in September 1978. As a taster of things to come they also sent a very dry textbook for my perusal, and requested that I make a collection of descriptions and notes on twelve species of trees, to be handed in during the first week of term. I began to wonder what I had let myself in for!

4

The three-year Kew Diploma course was highly structured, with a different three months of each year spent in full-time lectures. We studied landscape design, landscape construction, systematic and structural botany, arboriculture, management, propagation and crop protection. For the rest of each year we worked three or six month stints in the various sections and departments of the Living Collections Division. In the Alpine Department, I worked in the alpine house, the woodland garden, the decorative nursery (growing plants for the bedding schemes) and in the grass garden. In the Tropical Department I worked in the display houses and in the tropical plant nursery, in the Temperate Department I spent six months in the newly restored Temperate House helping with landscaping and replanting. I also worked in the Arboretum, in Technical Glass (growing plants for the botanists and scientists to study), in the Planning Unit (producing information panels and leaflets) and in the Services Section (driving tractors, making compost and servicing machinery).

Whilst working from eight in the morning until four in the afternoon each day, we were expected to complete a series of written projects in our spare time (taxonomy, management, plant propagation and crop protection), together with keeping a vegetable plot and completing a pressed weed collection. On Monday evenings, we had to attend a plant identification test, identifying twenty plants collected from a different area of the gardens each week. In addition, I managed to fit in two student exchange visits, two weeks at Edinburgh Botanic Garden and three weeks at Leiden Botanic Garden in the Netherlands.

The students at Kew were amongst the most highly motivated people I have ever met. Many were mature students, determined to complete the course with the highest marks possible; some were overseas students, from France, Japan, New Zealand and Singapore; about a third of them were women (quite unusual at that time). What they all had in common was a desire to learn and a deeply rooted love of plants.

For me, the best thing about being at Kew was working with such an amazing range of plants. I have never found it easy to remember plant names, but being able to work with so many different kinds, in so many different conditions, made it seem much easier. It's difficult to say which was my favourite section to work in, but I did visit the temperate fern houses regularly – because they smelt of the Lake District in summer!

5

When I finished the Kew course in August 1981, I was awarded the Kew Diploma with honours, and suddenly I needed a job! I wanted to swap the bustle of London for a peaceful horticultural retreat in the country, to be a Head Gardener on a private estate. The problem was that no self-respecting owner of a country estate was going to entrust their garden to a young, untested, female with no experience in managing staff. Fair point – apart from the gender bit. In the nick of time two Supervisors' posts at Kew became vacant, and students were encouraged to apply for them in order to build up their managerial experience.

I applied to be Supervisor of the newly restored Temperate House, a huge range of cool greenhouses that is often overlooked in favour of the more famous Palm House at Kew. Designed by Decimus Burton and built between 1860 and 1899 at a cost of £29,000, the Temperate House shelters plants from all over the temperate world. In 1981 it was in the final stages of a seven-year restoration that had cost many times the original construction bill. The folk at Kew obviously thought they knew me better than the naturally suspicious country estate owners; they gave me the job and put me in charge of two members of staff and two students! Dropped in at the deep end, we had just a few months to finish the replanting and labelling, and to get the whole place shipshape before it was officially reopened by the Queen.

The Temperate House holds collections from South Africa, New Zealand, Australia, the Mediterranean, the Himalayas, Africa, Mexico, Brazil, Chile, Hawaii, China, Japan and India, together with collections of proteas, tender rhododendrons, tree ferns, and temperate fruits such as oranges, lemons, olives, lychees and tree-tomatoes. There is a main, central block, complete with balcony for looking down on the plants, and two smaller wings, linked to the central block by octagons. I had my first office in the basement of the South Octagon, which also houses a staff room and a boiler house. The basement of the North Octagon held another boiler house and a small exhibition. The whole range was over 160 metres long and housed around 3000 plants. That's a lot of Latin names to learn!

During my time in the Temperate Section I went on a tour of the large glasshouses of Europe, visiting Botanic and private gardens in France, Germany, Belgium and Switzerland. Kew also assisted me on a visit to the Everglades in Florida.

6

After three years in the Temperate House, I began to get itchy feet; the lure of that country estate was beginning to make itself felt again! At about the same time the post of Supervisor of the Orchid Unit became vacant. The Deputy Curator approached me and asked if I would like a transfer – they needed either an orchid expert or an experienced supervisor to fill the post. At first I was very doubtful of my ability to do the job; what I knew about orchids could have been written on a postage stamp! However the Unit was blessed with a talented grower, David Menzies, who helped me with the plants, and I was already familiar with the idiosyncratic ways of Kew itself; I soon began to feel at home. Only another 3,000 plant names to learn!

One of the most exciting things I did during this time was to take a month-long trip to Mexico to study orchids in the wild. Sponsored by the Sainsbury Orchid Foundation, I visited orchid growers in Mexico City, and Oaxaca on the west side of the country, and stayed for a time at the Botanic Gardens in Xalapa on the east coast. The people I met were wonderful, welcoming and helpful in the extreme, the countryside and the plants I saw were unforgettable (apart from the names!)

Whilst I worked in the Orchid Unit I lived in a flat nearby, in the servants quarters of Kew Palace. My address was flat 2, Kew Palace, quite a step up from my previous bedsit in Chiswick High Road! The flat had a garden attached and I was able to keep my first dog, a Bedlington-lurcher called Finn. Later we were joined by my brother who persuaded me that we needed Meg, a lurcher from a rescue centre in Kingston, to keep Finn company whilst we were at work. Since Finn disliked Meg from the moment she arrived, this plan backfired somewhat, but both dogs remained my companions for the next 13 years. The only plants that survived in the garden with the dogs were a bed of nerines, a venerable apple tree and a drunken eucalyptus that I tried to cut down and remove. It refused to die and kept sprouting up from the base each spring, forming a rather attractive thicket of juvenile foliage. In more recent years I have tried to coppice eucalyptus on purpose to keep them small and young; they have almost invariably died – perhaps I am cursed by that original tree?

7

After three years in the Orchid Unit, my feet began to itch again; that Head Gardener's post on a country estate was still calling to me! I began to read the job adverts in Horticulture Week, looking for a new job away from the noise and bustle of London. I was particularly interested in working in Cumbria, having spent many holidays walking on the fells with family and friends, in the Wasdale area in particular. Finally, after several months of looking, an advert appeared from the Lake District Special Planning Board (as it was then) seeking a Head Gardener for the Lake District National Park Centre at Brockhole (as it was then). The pay was less than that of a Supervisor at Kew, but there was a house with the job and what price all that fresh air and stress-free living? I duly applied for the post and was invited for an interview in March 1987.

Staying at my sister's house in Redditch the night before, the windscreen of my car cracked on the motorway just north of Birmingham. The faster I drove, the larger the crack got. I arrived late and flustered, wearing my best suit and having neglected to bring a raincoat – needless to say it rained all day. I can clearly recall standing on the jetty after my interview (under a large, borrowed umbrella) gazing at the clear water and watching a pair of swans cruising by, deciding that this would be a Good Place to live and work. While other candidates were interviewed, I sat in my car waiting for the Autoglass man to arrive. Sylvia Watthews came down to the car park from the offices (under another large umbrella) to say the interview panel wanted to see me again; to my delight they wanted to offer me the job...

By the beginning of May I had packed up my London life, said goodbye to my friends at Kew and moved to Brockhole. The Lodge was still being decorated when I arrived, the gardens had been without a Head Gardener for six months and the weeds had not been slow to take advantage. The gardens at Brockhole were originally designed for the Gaddum family by Thomas Mawson at the turn of the last century. Although there have been changes in path surfacing and planting styles over the last 100 years, the layout and construction of the paths, walls and borders remain largely as Mawson left them. The juggling act facing me as the new Head Gardener was to conserve and retain this historical perspective whilst producing a garden fit and strong enough to enhance a modern visitor centre with thousands of visitors each year.

8

Working with two established gardeners, David Hulse and Adrian Gigg, my first few years at Brockhole were spent rescuing and rejuvenating the gardens. Because I insisted on starting around the House and working outwards; doing each bed properly, taking out over-mature or unsuitable plantings, weeding thoroughly, replanting and mulching thickly; some areas got much worse before they got better! There were many critics and for several years we had to live with the reputation that Brockhole gardens were only horticulturally interesting when the rhododendrons were flowering.

Encouraged and supported by our boss David Thomas, Area Manager for the south-east of the National Park, we slowly began to see the light at the end of the tunnel. The gardens looked neater, and as the things we planted became established there were interesting and unusual plants to see all year round. We made links with other gardens and gardeners at Levens Hall, Sizergh Castle, Lingholm, Holehird, Acorn Bank and Brantwood, exchanging plants and information. My former colleagues at Kew sent a vanload of surplus woodland plants and some exotic plants for the Orangery; and Keith Parker, a former Kew student now working at Kew's satellite garden Wakehurst Place, sent surplus seedlings and plantlets from Sussex. Other friends sent plants from Ventnor and Edinburgh Botanic Gardens.

Helped by other members of National Park staff, BTCV, Voluntary Wardens, Manpower Services and a string of volunteers, we put up a pergola and trellis, resurrected the kitchen garden, started the wildflower meadow, planted new areas of woodland and dozens of specimen trees. We were able to produce a gardens leaflet, take regular garden walks and open

the gardens and grounds for the whole twelve months of the year.

During these early years I lived in the Head Gardener's Lodge at Brockhole, with the gardens and grounds as my back yard. It was lovely to be able to stroll round in the early mornings and evenings, down through the gardens to the wood and lakeshore. In 1988 Keith Parker and I were married, though we did not manage to live together before or even after we were wed! We thought for a while that I should move down to Sussex, perhaps setting up a landscape design and construction business, but a few weekends spent walking on the fells convinced Keith that we should stay in Cumbria. He got a job in Barrow and moved up in March 1989. In January 1990 our son Michael was born at Helme Chase in Kendal, and our family was complete.

9

In late 1990, Keith took on a new job based in Whitehaven. This meant a round trip for him of over a hundred miles each day, so we had to think about moving house. Threlkeld and Keswick are approximately half way between Brockhole and Whitehaven, but the houses there were either too expensive or not suitable for dogs and small children. Just as we were beginning to despair we found the ideal cottage at Stanthwaite, next to Uldale, on the edge of the Caldbeck fells.

Having lived at Brockhole, residing in the countryside was not quite new territory for us, but Uldale was a completely different experience. For a start it was quiet, no A591 running past the front drive, though tractors and livestock make their own kind of noises! For the first time we had neighbours, (there were three other houses in our little hamlet) and cows came up and down the lane for milking twice a day. The surrounding countryside was lovely, with views to the Solway in one direction and the slopes of Skiddaw in the other. There were foxes and hares in the fields, with nesting curlews, lapwings and buzzards close by.

Our back garden was tiny, just a strip of land ten or twelve feet wide along the length of the cottage, but it was bounded by a picket fence on the other side of which were open fields that stretched all the way to the coast. The plants here not only had to be very hardy, they had to be able to withstand the strong winds that blew across the fields from the sea. We grew euphorbias, *Erysimum, Primula auricula, Iris sibirica*, geraniums, crocosmias and tough shrubs like berberis, *Rosa rugosa*, buddleia and willows. Our front garden was even tinier, simply a raised strip about three feet wide along the length of the cottage. Anything that grew here had to be able to withstand a twice-daily grazing from passing cows; after much experimentation we settled for tough, low-growing alpines.

It's a little-known fact that professional gardeners tend not to do much gardening away from work. Although I am quite happy to provide seeds and cuttings from time to time, and to offer helpful suggestions and unasked-for advice, Keith has always been the Head Gardener at home. I tell him it's a good antidote to too much office work! For me the garden at home is not for working in, but for sitting in the sun admiring the plants.

10

After living at Uldale for three years we moved, almost unintentionally, to Cockermouth. Whilst visiting friends one Saturday we noticed a large, slightly scruffy, three-storey terrace house with a For Sale sign outside. Finding ourselves at a loose end the following weekend, we decided to have a look around. The house needed a little maintenance on the fabric and a great deal of decorating, but it had Victorian ceiling roses, cornicing, and a proper vestibule like my grandma used to have, with an etched glass door into the hall. How could we resist? It seemed huge after our little cottage and we were definitely in need of room to stretch ourselves.

The garden at the front of our new house was about twenty feet square, a rectangle of lawn with an overgrown, dwarf conifer at each corner. One of our first jobs was to remove three of these small trees; digging them out and unblocking the surface water drains that their roots had clogged was an excellent way of meeting all the neighbours – everyone stopped for a chat! Although we have since planted the borders with more suitable and interesting plants the lawn and borders remain relatively unchanged. When gardens are close together, as they are in a terrace, they look better if they are similar to each other rather than with one standing out by being radically different from the rest.

The garden at the back is a yard! There are several distinct advantages to a yard over a back garden, not the least of which is that the grass never needs mowing. There is always paving under your feet, a bonus when hanging out the washing or riding a bicycle, and there is no mud to traipse into the house. Actually we have the best of both worlds because we have a long narrow bed the length of the yard and about six feet wide. We are able to grow flowers here, with climbers along the wall behind. In addition Keith has a large number of plants in pots, which he rotates around the yard, putting those in flower and looking at their best in front of the kitchen window, by the back door or next to the seating area.

Cockermouth is a comfortable, friendly, working town with a regular cattle market and not too many tourists. Michael has grown up here, his school is just down the road from our house, his friends and ours live nearby. Although I have quite a long drive to work, it only takes between forty-five minutes and an hour – there are plenty of people working in cities who spend longer than this commuting, and I get to drive through some of the most beautiful scenery in the country!

11

The results of too much decorating, together with years of bending and stretching in the garden, began to surface in 1997. I suffered a series of disc and facet-joint problems in my back that culminated in my having to take six months off work. On my return it was agreed that I should work only three days a week, and not do any energetic gardening!

This has proved quite frustrating, but the two days a week that I have free are a real bonus! I have been able to spend more time with Michael, help out with his school garden and resurrect my half-finished Open University degree. Our two Lurchers have passed away but I keep fit(ish) by walking Chloe, our English bull terrier. Having written occasional articles for the *Westmorland Gazette* in the past, I was delighted when, in July 1998, Joanne Colley approached me with a proposal for regular work. Since their previous gardening writer had retired they were looking for someone to fill the gap, producing a weekly article that readers of the Gazette would find interesting, useful and relevant to their own part of the country. With some trepidation I agreed to give it a try.

It has been a fascinating experience. I have to produce an article each week, with a couple of slides or photographs to illustrate it, for 52 weeks each year. So far I have managed for nearly three years, but it is not easy to think of a new topic each week. In addition the articles have to be written a couple of weeks in advance of publication, so I have to consider what will be interesting or flowering in the next few weeks, not easy, particularly when a picture is needed. A few times I have written that some plant is looking spectacular, only to find that by the time the article appears the plant has gone over! At other times I've wanted to write about a plant that is flowering but have had no picture to illustrate it, so I take a picture of it and put the article on the back boiler for twelve months. Occasionally I have had a great photo, but not much to say about the plant, so I introduce it into the article as an aside, which gives me the chance to use the picture!

I am always enormously flattered, and not a little embarrassed, when visitors to Brockhole tell me they have been reading the *Westmorland Gazette* articles. I hope it may be interesting for them to be able to come to the gardens and see for themselves what I have been writing about.

12

Over the last 14 years the gardens at Brockhole have changed and yet not changed. The skeleton of paths, beds, hedges, lawns, woods and pasture have remained the same, whilst the plants and plantings have become softer, more varied and I hope more interesting. The gardens are quite different at different seasons. I can never decide if I prefer spring, when everything is bursting into life after the dreary winter months, or autumn, when the leaves are such brilliant colours and it's almost time to put the gardens to bed for the winter.

The wildlife and birds have continued to visit, in some cases in greater numbers than before, though sadly we have seen the disappearance of red squirrels and the establishment of greys. I have yet to see a badger at Brockhole, but others have and there is plenty of evidence of their nightly foraging! Huge numbers of human visitors have passed through the gardens and grounds, around 170,000 in an average year. Many find the time to stop and chat, and I know that many appreciate the changes we have made. I especially enjoy meeting the visitors who come back every year, sometimes several times a year, to see how work is progressing. National Park Staff have come and gone, and I find to my surprise that I am the longest-serving member of staff at Brockhole. Gardeners are amongst those who stay the longest; oddly, without seeming to try, the garden exerts some sort of hold over us, keeping us here almost in spite of ourselves. The two gardeners I started out with have gone, replaced by Sue Lee, who has worked with me for eleven years, and David Ostle, who has been at Brockhole for eight years. More recently we have been joined by Rose Wolfe, a Cumbrian who had been working for the National Trust for Scotland at Culzean Castle in Ayrshire.

The work is never finished. I read somewhere that gardens are either moving forwards or they are moving backwards, it is impossible to stand still. Our latest projects include working towards a bid to the Heritage Lottery Fund. The terrace walls need some repairing, the Orangery could do with a new heating system, we must have improved access for visitors with disabilities and we would like better signing and interpretation throughout the gardens. One of the most interesting parts of the bid will be the restoration of the Edwardian irrigation system for the gardens, huge rainwater tanks beneath the ground outside the Orangery, fed and filled from the roof and gutters of the main house. The tanks feed pipes and taps throughout the gardens, long since defunct. I hope I will be at Brockhole long enough to see them put back into action!

Index